BADGE OF HONOR

My Stand for the West Philippine Sea

Sen. Francis Tolentino

Published by Tolentino Maritime Publications

First printed in the United States of America by Amazon KDP, 2026.

To the Filipino people, and to all nations and peoples who draw courage from islands, wisdom from the oceans, and justice from the law of the sea – this book stands for you.

Contents

INTRODUCTION

On October 12, 2025, three small ships from the Philippine Bureau of Fisheries and Aquatic Resources (BFAR) were anchored near Sandy Cay, a reef a few nautical miles from the tiny island of Pag-asa in the West Philippine Sea. Pag-asa is part of the Philippine Kalayaan Island Group, a collection of small islands, cays, reefs and shoals. Known to sailors for centuries as a place of danger and shipwreck, the Kalayaan Island Group forms part of the larger Spratly Islands archipelago, named after the nineteenth-century British whaling captain, Richard Spratly.

Captain Spratly spent much of a long career at sea hunting whales in what he called "the southern part of the China Sea", around the Philippines, Indonesia and Malaysia. In 1843, as he wrote in a letter to *The Nautical Magazine And Naval Chronicle,*[1] he spotted "two dangers" from his ship, *Cyrus*: two semi-submerged features on which a ship could founder. One he identified as "Ladd's Reef", in recognition of the fact that a Captain Ladd of the ship *Austen* was thought to have been the first to have spotted the hazard. The other, he called "Spratly's Sandy Island" – a term which would later be given to all of the Spratly Islands archipelago.

The Kalayaan Island Group lies between roughly 150 and 280 nautical miles (nm) west of Palawan – its nearest features fall well within the Philippines' 200nm Exclusive Exclusion Zone (EEZ), while its administrative center at Pag-asa Island is some 280nm from Puerto Princesa.

Another major group of islands, reefs and shoals, known as the Scarborough Shoals, lies to the north of the Spratlys, about 130nm west-to-northwest of the Philippine capital of Manila. They were also named after a merchant vessel from the previous century, HMS *Scarborough*, which was chartered by the British East India Company to transport tea between China and the British East Indies. The ship was heading for China when it foundered on a reef. The crew threw canons overboard and emptied water casks to lighten the ship and tried to pull her free using anchored longboats, but the *Scarborough* stuck firm.

The ship was eventually lifted off the rocks by the tide, and finally made harbor at Whampoa, near Canton, China, on September 21, 1748. Despite the widespread subsequent international use of the name, "Scarborough Shoal", the reefs and shoals had been previously identified in a 1734 Philippine map and called "Panacot" – a Filipino word for "threat" or "scary place." They were re-named in an official survey carried out in 1800 by the nation's colonial Spanish rulers, as "Bajo de Masinloc" ("the shoal of Masinloc" – a coastal town northwest of Manila). Filipinos today still call the region "Bajo de Masinloc" or "Panatag Shoal" – meaning "tranquil" or "undisturbed," probably reflecting the use of the shoal as a shelter from typhoons; the shoal had come to be seen less as a hazard and more as a well-known fishing destination and even a shelter from bad weather.

(Photo shows Author with his original 1820 and 1835 maps depicting Scarborough Shoal)

Bajo de Masinloc and the Kalayaan Island Group are, and have always been, hazards to shipping. To Filipinos, they have also been a hugely important source of food: the Bajo de Masinloc is home to more than 200 species of fish, including tuna, mackerel, croaker, anchovies, shrimp and the highly prized grouper and snapper. The "coral gardens" of the region are home to giant clams, sea cucumbers and green sea turtles, all of which are protected rare species. The Kalayaan Island Group is particularly rich in coral, harboring around one third of all the coral reefs in the world's oceans, providing a vital breeding ground for the whole of the West Philippine Sea and representing one of the most biodiverse reef systems on the planet.

Which brings us back to the Philippine BFAR fisheries vessels anchored off Pag-asa in October 2025.

Pag-asa island is home to a tiny community of a few hundred Filipinos, nearly all of whom make a living from fishing, using the traditional *bangka* fishing boats – narrow wooden boats with outriggers on each side for stability. Larger fishing vessels make the long trip to Pag-asa from Puerto Princesa and spend many weeks at sea to make their trips profitable. Because of the importance of the fishing industry to the Philippines as a whole, the fishing fleet is resupplied at sea by BFAR vessels, bringing fuel, food, medicines and the ice needed to preserve the catches in the ships' holds.

On the morning of October 12th, 2025, the sea was calm, and a weak sun broke through a light covering of cloud. The three anchored BFAR vessels were approached by a Chinese Coastguard (CCG) vessel, bow number 21559, accompanied by a fleet of what reports of the incident call "suspected militia vessels." These are privately registered fishing vessels believed to be part of the Chinese People's Armed Forces Maritime Militia, an organized, trained and government-subsidized body operating under the command of the People's Liberation Army of China. The militia vessels carry out normal fishing activities, but they can also be used to harass and intimidate Philippine fishing vessels and those of other nations fishing in the South China Sea, while allowing the Chinese government to deny official responsibility, referring typically to "so-called militia vessels."

The Chinese ships arrived off Pag-asa and began what Philippine Coastguard Commodore Jay Tarriela described later that day as "dangerous and provocative maneuvers" close to the Philippine vessels.[2] At around 9.15 a.m., the CCG vessel – a far more powerful ship, about three times the size of the BFAR vessels – switched on its water cannons, threatening the Philippine vessels. The ships' water cannons fire a dense jet of water at high speed, powerful enough to buckle steel railings, smash bridgehouse windows and send sailors crashing into bulkheads or even overboard. The huge volumes of water can also, of course, wreck navigation and other electronic equipment and heating and ventilation systems.

As the BFAR vessels weighed anchor and moved away, they were followed by the CCG vessel. The Chinese ship pursued one BFAR vessel, the *Datu Pagbuaya*, passing close by, with its siren blaring, raking the length of the *Pagbuaya's* deck with water from its cannon. As the Philippine vessel turned away to starboard, the Chinese vessel turned full circle in the opposite direction, approaching the *Pagbuaya* once more from behind, ramming the BFAR vessel's stern and forcing it to one side as the Chinese ship ploughed on. There were no injuries to the *Pagbuaya's* crew, and the ship was later reported to have suffered minor structural damage.

In a press statement after the incident, Commodore Tarriela said, "Despite these bullying tactics and aggressive actions, the Philippine coast guard and the Bureau of

Fisheries and Aquatic Resources remain resolute. We will not be intimidated or driven away, as our presence in the Kalayaan Island Group is crucial for protecting the rights and livelihoods of Filipino fishermen."[3]

The CCG's version of events was very different. A spokesperson, Liu Dejun, said that the Philippine vessel had ignored "repeated stern warnings from the Chinese side and dangerously approached" the CCG vessel. "Full responsibility lies with the Philippine side," Liu continued.[4] In April 2025, CCG officers had planted a Chinese flag on Sandy Cay. The Philippine Coastguard responded a few days later by raising the Philippine flag on the Cay, which the CCG declared was an "illegal" act. The CCG went on to say that China had "indisputable sovereignty" over all of the Spratly Islands, including Sandy Cay, [5] a remarkable claim that we will explore in subsequent chapters.

America was swift to condemn China's actions. "The United States condemns China's October 12 ramming and water cannoning of a Philippine Bureau of Fisheries and Aquatic Resources vessel close to Thitu Island [Pag-asa] in the South China Sea," said a US State Department spokesperson, Thomas Piggott. "We stand with our Philippine allies as they confront China's dangerous actions which undermine regional stability." He went on to say that "China's sweeping territorial and maritime claims in the South China Sea and its increasingly coercive actions to advance them at the expense of its neighbors" were a threat to regional stability and "fly in the facc of its prior commitments to resolve disputes peacefully."[6]

In 1951, the US and the Philippines entered a mutual defense treaty which, as Piggott went on to highlight in his statement, commits the US to a military response if the

Philippines' experience "armed attacks on Philippine armed forces, public vessels, or aircraft – including those of its Coast Guard – anywhere in the South China Sea." The CCG vessel's water-cannon attack and subsequent ramming of the *Datu Pagbuaya* were carefully calibrated to fall short of an "armed" attack.

***

The waters of Sandy Cay, where the Philippine vessels were anchored, are just 1.6nm to 1.8nm off Pag-asa, well within the Philippine island's internationally defined 12nm territorial seas.

Sandy Cay lies between Pag-asa and an artificial island the Chinese have constructed on the nearby Subi Reef, complete with an airstrip, military structures and storage facilities. The sheltered waters within the artificial structures provide shelter for Chinese vessels – some of which formed part of the flotilla that attacked the *Datu Pagbuaya* and its sister vessels. The artificial, militarized island on Subi Reef is also within the Philippines' 200nm EEZ. Because it is constructed on a reef – a "low-tide elevation" that is completely submerged at low tide – and is not an island, it does not generate its own territorial sea. And, unless China can in some way prove its remarkable claim to "Indisputable sovereignty" over all of the Spratly Islands, it is illegally occupying Subi Reef and other features in the Spratlys. And yet China feels able to declare that the Philippine vessels, legally anchored in their own waters off Sandy Cay, were in some way intruding into what they claim are Chinese waters.

How did we get to this point?

The rest of this book is an account of my part in the fight against China's illegal efforts to lay claim to vast swathes of the South China Sea, and of the legal and political efforts to assert the Philippines' rights to its own territorial waters and to its wider EEZ and continental shelf.

After the October 12 incident, Philippine coast guard commandant Admiral Ronnie Gil Gavan said, "The harassment we faced today only strengthens our resolve. Filipino fisherfolk depend on these waters and neither water cannons nor ramming will deter us from fulfilling our commitment (…) to not surrender a square inch of our territory to any foreign power."[7]

I wholeheartedly agree with Admiral Gavan. As a Senator of the Philippines, I was the principal author of the Philippine Maritime Zones Act, which was passed by the Philippine Congress in 2024. The Act defines and asserts the Philippines' rights and entitlements to all its maritime zones, in accordance with the ruling of a 2016 tribunal in the Hague, convened under the United Nations Convention on the Law of the Sea (UNCLOS), which found that China's "historic claims" to these territories were unfounded and incompatible with UNCLOS.

As a result of the passing of this Act, I was subsequently banned from ever entering China, something I wear as the "badge of honor" which is the title of this book.

CHAPTER 1

Mischief on Mischief Reef

Mischief Reef, or Panganiban Reef as it is known to Filipinos, lies around 129 nautical miles (nm) west of Palawan Island in the Philippine's Kalayaan Island Group and just over 100nm southeast of Pag-asa Island, which we encountered in the Introduction to this book. The reef is well within the Philippines 200nm Exclusive Economic Zone (EEZ) as defined by the United Nations Convention on the Law of the Sea (UNCLOS), a body of law often referred to as "The Constitution of the Sea," which clearly sets out each nation's rights to its surrounding waters. Within its 200nm EEZ, for example, a nation has exclusive rights to "explore and exploit, and the responsibility to conserve and manage, both living and non-living resources."[8] UNCLOS, the concept of EEZs and various other legally defined concepts such as a nation's 12nm "territorial waters" are central to this book, and we will explore them in more detail later.

Mischief Reef is an almost perfect circle of coral, around 5.5 miles in diameter, surrounding a central lagoon. The whole reef is submerged at high tide. There are two narrow channels through the reef into the lagoon, making it a useful refuge for fishing boats in bad weather – if you are an experienced sailor and know the waters well. Otherwise,

Mischief Reef, like nearly all the reefs, shoals and cays in the region, is a hazard to shipping, which is why this area in the east of the Spratly Islands is known as "Dangerous Ground." The only visitors to Mischief Reef are fishermen.

In January 1995, the Philippine fishing vessel *Analita* was sailing close to the reef when, to their great astonishment, they saw that four large platforms, each supporting several octagonal concrete bunkers, had been constructed on stilts raised above the reef itself. They were even more surprised to find themselves quickly surrounded by what turned out to be Chinese vessels and to learn that they were being forcibly detained. They were held captive for a week and then released, having promised not to tell the Philippine authorities about their surprise discovery. It was a promise they did not keep; on their return to Palawan, they told anyone who would listen about their experiences and confusing discovery.[9] The Philippine authorities struggled to make sense of the news. The mayor of Pag-asa was instructed by the government to visit the reef, but his boat was driven away by Chinese vessels.[10]

Philippine navy vessels and an Air Force plane were sent to verify the fishermen's reports, and eventually aerial photographs of the mysterious structures were successfully taken. The Philippine government lodged a formal diplomatic protest with Beijing.

At first, the Chinese Foreign ministry denied that any structures had been built on the reef or that they had been occupied. When presented with photographs of the structures and nearby Chinese vessels, they said that the structures were merely shelters for Chinese fishermen, and that Filipino fishermen and those of other nations would be able to use them at a later date.[11] There was also a suggestion from Beijing that the structures may have been built on the orders of "low-level functionaries without the knowledge and consent of the Chinese government."[12] This seemed highly unlikely, given the scale of the resources that had would have to be mobilized to carry out such an impressive construction project. The myth was dispelled on March 10, 1995, when the Chinese Foreign Minister, Qian Qichen, made this statement, confirming that the operation had taken place with the full knowledge of China's political leadership: "Ours is not a military activity and will pose no threat to other countries. Chinese fishermen have been traditionally fishing in the region and shelters have been built to protect them. China has had sovereignty over the islands since ancient times and there were no disputes. Just in the late 70s, some countries made claims over the islands. China has shown restraint and is willing to develop the region in a co-operative way, setting aside disputes."[13]

The statement was to prove a model for subsequent similar operations: announce baldly that China's sovereignty in the region has existed "since ancient times"; reassure concerned neighbors that China's intentions were peaceful and offer the suggestion of future "cooperation" – but a cooperation that was now based on China's *de facto* occupation of the disputed territory.

Later in March, the Philippine Under Secretary to the Foreign Office, Rodolfo Severino, led a delegation of Filipino officials to Beijing for talks, but with little success. "The Chinese continued to maintain their position that these structures are wind shelters for their fishermen," Severino said after the meetings.[14] The Association of Southeast Asian Nations (ASEAN) issued a joint statement expressing "serious concern" about the development and calling for all parties to show restraint and seek for a peaceful resolution.

The occupation of Mischief Reef was the first time that China had occupied a maritime feature belonging to a member of ASEAN – in this case, the Philippines. China had a long previous history of conflict with Vietnam, which would not become a member of ASEAN until 1995. That conflict was over the Paracel Islands, which lie over 400nm north of the Spratly Islands, roughly equidistant from central Vietnam and southern China, straddling the border of both countries' EEZs. There had been skirmishes between China and Vietnam in the Paracels as far back as 1956, at the end of the First Indochina War between France and the Việt Minh. France had been the colonial power in the region since the formal establishment of French Indochina in 1887, though they had shared power with the Japanese during World War II and briefly ceded all control to Japan in1945, not long before the Japanese surrender. In the course of the war, Japan had also taken control of both the Spratlys and the Paracels.

In the 1951 San Francisco Peace Treaty which ended the war, Japan renounced all claim to both groups of islands – but the treaty did not address the issue of which nations would inherit sovereignty. When France withdrew its troops from the Paracels after its failed attempt to regain control of northern Vietnam from the nationalist movement, leading to the partitioning of Vietnam into the Democratic Republic of Vietnam ("North Vietnam") and the Republic of Vietnam ("South Vietnam"), China quietly occupied the more northerly Amphitrite Group of islands before South Vietnamese troops could arrive, leaving South Vietnam able to regain later control of only the Crescent Group of islands to the southwest.

In 1973, Chinese fishing vessels began operations in the Crescent Group, leading to clashes with vessels from the South Vietnamese navy. In January 1974, a South Vietnamese frigate fired warning shots at two Chinese fishing vessels entering the area and shelled a Chinese flag that had been planted on one of the islands. The frigate was joined by three other South Vietnamese navy vessels, and troops were landed to remove Chinese flags on two islands. China dispatched a total of six ships to the Crescent group to confront the South Vietnamese, resulting in a naval battle, with sailors killed and injured on both sides. China emerged the victor and quickly garrisoned the Paracels with troops. The man in charge of the garrisoning was Liu Huaqing, then deputy chief of staff of China's navy, the People's Liberation Army Navy (PLAN).[15] Liu was appointed by Deng Xiaoping, Chairman of the Central Military Commission, who had emerged as China's effective leader following the death of Mao Zedong in 1976. Deng and Liu were comrades from the earliest day of the Chinese Communist Party and the Chinese Civil War.

In 1982, Liu was made commander of the PLAN. He oversaw a dramatic shift in Chinese naval strategy, to the extent that today he is known as "the father of the modern Chinese Navy." Liu spent most of his early military career in the People's Liberation Army (PLA), and although some experts throw doubt on whether Liu himself, essentially an "Army man," was the architect of that naval strategy, he is unquestionably the person who was responsible for building a modern Chinese navy powerful enough to execute the strategy China had devised.

Since its establishment in the late 1940s, the PLAN had been focused on coastal defense, firstly against a possible amphibious attack by the defeated Nationalists of the Republic of China (ROC), who had retreated to Taiwan after their defeat by the People's Republic of China (PRC) in the Civil War. Later, as the threat from the ROC receded, PLAN's predominant role was to offer support to the army, protecting vital sea lanes and harassing a land-based enemy from the sea with artillery and naval planes – from the Sino-Soviet split of the early 1960s until the fall of the Soviet Union in 1991, China's main fear had been of a land invasion from the north by the USSR.

In the late 1980s the PLAN's strategy moved from Coastal Defense, or "brown water" defense (*jin'an fangyu*), to Offshore Defense, or "green water" defense (*jinhai fangyu*): the ability to protect China's interests in its wider surrounding waters.

China's coastline is hemmed in (from a Chinese perspective) by a chain of island nations: Japan to the northeast, Taiwan to the east, and the Philippines to the southeast. In China's developing, more outward-looking naval strategy, this gave rise to the concept of a "First Island Chain" stretching from Japan in the north to Indonesia in the south and looping back north to Vietnam – the boundaries of an area that encompasses the East China Sea and the South China Sea and, of course, all of the Spratly and Paracel Islands. There was also the concept of "blue water" defense – the Pacific Ocean off the eastern coasts of Japan, Taiwan and the Philippines, and of a "Second Island Chain" of defense, stretching from Japan's home island of Honshu to New Guinea, via the Mariana Islands (which include the US territory of Guam).

According to David Hartnett, researcher for the CAN (Center for Naval Analyses) Corporation, writing for the Center for International Maritime Security, Huaqing understood that to deliver the Offshore Defense strategy, the PLAN would need to develop four capabilities: "the ability to seize limited sea control in certain areas for a certain period of time; the ability to effectively defend China's sea lanes; the ability to fight outside China's claimed maritime areas; and the ability to implement a credible nuclear deterrent." Huaqing's great achievement was in persuading the government of the need to commit the resources to achieve these capabilities. Hartnett argues that it was only in the 1970s that Beijing became aware of the economic, as well as the strategic, benefits for controlling these maritime areas: the potential to exploit hydrocarbons and minerals in the seabed, the growing importance of fisheries to feed the nation, and the need to protect China's sea lanes as it began to develop the global exports that were to become so critical to the country's growing economic success.[16]

In the Spring of 1987, in Paris, a meeting of a relatively obscure scientific body was to have a dramatic and unforeseen impact on the future of the Spratly Islands and the South China Sea. The Intergovernmental Oceanographic Commission (IOC) of UNESCO (the United Nations Educational, Scientific and Cultural Organization) had met to discuss a new initiative, the Global Sea Level Observing System (GLOSS), that had been established two years earlier to monitor the potential effect of global warming on sea levels. A Chinese delegation attended and proposed that they could contribute to GLOSS by setting up tide gauges in both the East China Sea and on several maritime features in the Spratlys, describing these brazenly as China's "coasts" – as if the Spratlys, around 750nm from the nearest Chinese territory, could in any meaningful sense be described as China's "coast". China was given a charter to install the tide gauges, giving it scientific cover to establish a presence on various features in the Spratlys. A 2016 article in the *South China Post* reports that "UN [...] scientists later admitted they were unaware of the territorial disputes in the region."[17]

On his appointment as commander of the PLAN, Liu had emphasized the need to establish a presence in the Spratlys. The Central Military Commission gave Liu approval to occupy a total of nine reefs in the island group.[18] In 1987, Liu ordered the South Sea Fleet's first combat patrol in the South China Sea. In January 1988, Chinese forces occupied Kagitingan (Fiery Cross) Reef in the Spratlys, a group of three reefs on the western edge of the Dangerous Ground, using the setting up of an oceanic observation station as diplomatic cover, following the charter given to China by GLOSS the previous year.[19] The reef was chosen because it was large enough to build the proposed weather station, but more significantly because it was not actually occupied by any other nation, despite various claims of sovereignty, and because it was situated some distance from other disputed features. Vietnam immediately dispatched two cargo ships to the reef with construction materials to build structures of their own, but were driven away by PLAN vessels. Both Chinese and Vietnamese ships then approached Calderon (Cuarteron) Reef, 75nm southeast of Kagitingan (Fiery Cross) Reef. The Chinese fleet included a destroyer with escort and transport vessels, and Vietnam could only muster a minesweeper and an armed freighter. The outgunned Vietnamese ships withdrew.

Then, in March 1988, the Vietnamese navy sent three transport vessels carrying troops to three different features in the Pagkakaisa Bank (Union Banks), a drowned atoll east of Kagitingan (Fiery Cross) Reef, around 120nm west of the Philippines. The ships were destined for Roxas (Collins), Pagkakaisa (Lansdowne) and Mabini (Johnson South) Reefs, over all of which Vietnam claimed sovereignty, leading to a bloody confrontation.

Chinese and Vietnamese accounts of the ensuing battle vary. According to Vietnam, their soldiers, most of whom were unarmed, were transferring materials to the reef when three Chinese frigates arrived. In this account, the Vietnamese soldiers bravely gathered around the flag they had planted on the island and defended it against armed Chinese troops who had also landed on the reef. Some Vietnamese were killed, but their flag was not captured. The Chinese troops then withdrew, allowing the ships to open fire on the men gathered on the reef, killing or wounding all of them. Two of the Vietnamese vessels were sunk by Chinese fire, the third was deliberately run aground on Roxas (Collins) Reef to prevent its seizure by the Chinese.

According to China, there was a scuffle over the raised Vietnamese flags between Chinese and Vietnamese troops on the reef, during which the Vietnamese opened fire, forcing the Chinese troops to withdraw. Their frigate later opened fire on the Vietnamese troops on the reef. The Chinese frigate also fired on the accompanying Vietnamese transport vessel, causing it to catch fire and sink. Similar events occurred at Pagkakaisa (Lansdowne) Reef, according to China, where another Vietnamese vessel had landed a few troops. The Vietnamese opened fire on the approaching PLAN frigate, which fired back, sinking that transport vessel also.

Interestingly, a Chinese propaganda film made in 2009 to celebrate the 60th anniversary of the PLAN includes footage of the incident.[20] A YouTube video, posted by "Legends Lore" and titled "The 1988 Naval Battle: China's Victory at Chigua [Johnson South] Reef" shows an extract from the propaganda film that covers the incident.

The film's narrator claims *"a great victory"* for the PLAN at Chigua reef, with 300 Vietnamese casualties and nine Vietnamese captured, and only one Chinese sailor injured: shot in the arm when *"Vietnam fired the first shot."* The narrator explains the clash by saying that *"many of China's islands and reefs in the South China Sea [had been] illegally occupied by neighboring countries. To protect its maritime sovereignty, China boldly dispatched patrols to guard the islands and reefs."* The video shows footage filmed from Chinese vessels of a rather forlorn-looking group of Vietnamese troops standing knee-deep in water as the tide rises over a reef – presumably Mabini (Johnson South) Reef. The open boat that brought them to the reef can be seen with them, and it looks very much as though a flag is still flying over the reef, despite the Chinese narrator's claim that in a preceding scuffle on the reef, *"one of our soldiers [...] furiously tore down the flag"* that the Vietnamese had "*arrogantly hoisted.*" The Vietnamese soldiers do not seem to be carrying weapons; certainly not anything that would pose a threat to a Chinese frigate. In the grainy footage, the water around the Vietnamese soldiers suddenly erupts with great plumes of water from what looks like heavy machine gun fire – the waterspouts are too large for small arms fire – and everyone in the group quickly disappears under the water.[21] US Navy sources quote the number of Vietnamese deaths at seventy-four.[22]

At the end of the PLAN campaign, six of the originally-planned nine reefs in the Spratlys had been occupied: Kagitingan (Fiery Cross); Mabini (Johnson South); Zamora (Subi); Burgos (Gaven); McKennan (Hughes); and Calderon (Cuarteron), all previously claimed by Vietnam. By the end of 1988, China, despite the absence of any meaningful case for sovereignty in the Spratlys, had successfully occupied several of its maritime features. Deng Xiaoping sent his personal congratulations to the PLAN units.[23]

***

Over the coming years, China began to develop its occupied reefs, adding, for example, concrete platforms, communications facilities, lighthouses and garrisons for small numbers of troops. Vietnam nursed its wounds and its damaged pride. In the Philippines, there was deep uneasiness about the illegal occupation of reefs in the Kalayaan Island Group, but the overall situation remained relatively calm. Then, in 1992, China passed the Law of the People's Republic of China on the Territorial Sea and the Contiguous Zone, which explicitly claimed the Spratly Islands as Chinese territory and asserted that China's domestic maritime laws applied to these areas. This was a major escalation. There were also disputes, again between China and Vietnam, over oil exploration rights in disputed waters. China’s militarization of the occupied features in the Spratlys continued.

In 1992, ASEAN had issued its Declaration on the South China Sea (which was adopted in Manila and is also known as the Manila Declaration). The Declaration opened with an appeal for cooperation and restraint:

Recalling the historic, cultural and social ties that bind our peoples as states adjacent to the South China Sea; wishing to promote the spirit of kinship, friendship and harmony among our peoples who share similar Asian traditions and heritage; desirous of further promoting conditions essential to greater economic cooperation and growth; recognizing that we are bound by similar ideals of mutual respect, freedom, sovereignty and jurisdiction of the parties directly concerned; recognizing that South China Sea issues involve sensitive questions of sovereignty and jurisdiction of the parties directly concerned; [and] conscious that any adverse developments in the South China Sea directly affect peace and stability in the region...[24]

The declaration went on to call for the resolution of issues by peaceful means; for restraint and a positive climate for the resolution of disputes; and for cooperation on a wide range of vital common maritime concerns. It recommended the establishment of an international Code of Conduct for the South China Sea and called on all parties to subscribe to the declaration's principles. A Code of Conduct has yet to be crafted, even as Manila hosts the ASEAN summit in May 2026.

The 1995 occupation of Mischief Reef seemed to dash all these hopes of cooperation and peaceful resolution. The reef was indisputably within the EEZ of the Philippines, an ASEAN member. It was specifically listed in the Philippines 1978 Kalayaan decree – which formally incorporated the Kalayaan Island Group into Philippine territory as part of Palawan province – and there was no "scientific" pretext, such as the unfortunate fig leaf for the occupation of maritime features in the Spratlys given to China by UNESCO's GLOSS project. The notion that the structures on Mischief Reef were "fishermen's shelters" that would be made available to other fishermen was transparent nonsense (and subsequently quietly disappeared from statements by China about Mischief Reef). ASEAN, as we have seen, expressed its "serious concern."

The South China Sea had suddenly become a far more volatile and dangerous place.

CHAPTER 2

Lines in the Sea

China's occupation of Mischief Reef in 1995 had come at an interesting time, in geopolitical terms. In September 1991, following a wave of nationalist sentiment, the Philippine Senate had rejected the renewal of agreements with the US for its naval bases in the Philippines – bases that had been in place since 1947. This followed the unexpected volcanic eruption of Mount Pinatubo in Luzon in June 1991, which had already devastated the nearby US Clark Air Base and damaged the slightly more distant Subic Naval Base. The US withdrew its military from the Philippines in November 1992, lowering the American flag at Subic Bay for the last time. The Cold War had officially ended in December 1991 with the dissolution of the Soviet Union. China may have thought the time had come to test the political waters in the South China Sea in the new post-Cold War era, with a US military presence recently removed from the Philippines.

China's 1988 raids in the Spratly Islands had resulted in their occupation of six features: Kagitingan (Fiery Cross), Mabini (Johnson South), Zamora (Subi), Burgos (Gavin), McKennan (Hughes) and Caldera (Cuarteron) Reefs. There was limited development by China of these features for the next 18 years or so: communications equipment was put up, some concrete platforms were constructed and some garrisons and lighthouses were built. 1995 had seen the occupation of Panganiban (Mischief) Reef and the construction of the mysterious octagonal concrete structures on stilts.

In late 2013, development of all the occupied features suddenly escalated, on an alarming scale.

China dispatched a huge dredging vessel, capable of sucking 6000 cubic meters of material per hour from the seabed and piping it across distances of up to 15 kilometers. Sand, mud and coral debris were pumped onto the occupied reefs and concreted over, backfilling the reefs and raising them by several meters to create artificial islands. A Pentagon report estimated that by 2016, China had reclaimed 3,200 acres of land on the reefs.[25] The environmental damage was huge, destroying entire seabed ecological systems, smothering living coral with dredged materials and polluting surrounding waters with plumes of toxins.

What followed was a process of rapid militarization. By 2017, the reclaimed land on Panganiban (Mischief) Reef was home to a 3,000-metre runway; 24 combat aircraft hangars and 4 large hangars; 12 hardened missile shelters with retractable roofs to house surface-to-air (SAM) missiles; underground storage facilities; port facilities; and advanced communications and radar systems. Construction at Kagitingan (Fiery Cross) Reef and Zamora (Subi) Reef, followed a similar pattern, with 24 hangars capable of housing fighter jets, and four to five larger hangars capable of housing the largest aircraft in the Chinese fleet: bombers, transport planes, refueling tankers and surveillance aircraft. These three artificial islands have become known as "the

Big 3" Chinese-occupied artificial islands in the Spratlys. On the other China-occupied artificial islands, communications equipment, basic military structures and sometimes helipads were installed.[26, 27]

In 2015, the commander of the US Pacific Fleet, Admiral Harry B. Harris Jr., gave a speech to the Australian Strategic Policy Institute in Canberra, Australia, in which he described China's military activities in the Spratly and Paracel Islands as the construction of a "Great Wall of Sand". Referring to "China's pattern of provocative actions" towards other nations in the region and to "the lack of clarity on its sweeping nine-dash line claim that is inconsistent with international law," Harris urged "all claimants to conform to the 2002 China-ASEAN 'Declaration of Conduct,' where the parties committed to 'exercise self-restraint in the conduct of activities that would complicate or escalate disputes and affect peace and stability.'"[28]

Harris's reference to China's infamous "nine-dash line" is significant and goes to the heart of the issues discussed in this book.

The nine-dash line, also known as the U-shaped line, is exactly what it sounds like: nine dashes drawn on a map, that just so happen to encompass most of the South China Sea, including all of the significant maritime features, such as the Pratas Archipelago, situated roughly halfway between China and Taiwan, and the Paracel and Spratly Archipelagos. The disturbing reality is that this crude, hand-drawn line on a map has become a hugely significant issue in the geopolitics of the region.

China was vague about the precise meaning of the nine-dash line (hence Admiral Harris's reference to "lack of clarity"). The lines are geographically meaningless, since they have no coordinates and are hand drawn. The first dash, starting in the northeast, curves around the Batanes Islands – the northernmost province of the Philippines. The next line is off the coast of Luzon, the largest island of the Philippines. The third is to the northeast of Palawan, near the northernmost tip of the Spratly Islands. The fourth is very close to the southwestern tip of Palawan; the fifth is off the coast of Borneo. The next dash begins to curve back round to the northwest as the dashes carry on towards the eastern coast of Vietnam. The U-shaped line (also known as "the cow tongue line" in Vietnam, for obvious reasons) neatly "gathers in" all of the Spratly and Paracel Islands. "This all belongs to China", the line seems to pronounce, disregarding every other nation's territorial waters, Exclusive Economic Zones (EEZs) or sovereign claims to various features in the island groups.

China preferred to avoid explaining the precise meaning of the line, making use of "deliberate ambiguity" to avoid being challenged on the issue. Nevertheless, as we have seen, China talked often about its "historic claims" in the South China Sea and sometimes seemed to suggest that it did indeed have sovereign rights to all of the waters contained within the nine-dash line. This was a remarkable claim, since the area of sea enclosed by the line is estimated (remember that the line is imprecise) at around 2 million square kilometers – equivalent to more than one fifth of China's entire land mass, or about 80% of the Mediterranean Sea. The closest anyone had been able to get to China's official position seemed to be contained in its 2009 notes verbales (formal, unsigned diplomatic communications) to the UN, which said, "China has indisputable sovereignty over the islands in the South China Sea and the adjacent waters, and enjoys sovereign rights and jurisdiction over the relevant waters as well as the seabed and subsoil thereof."[29]

Putting to one side for the moment China's unsubstantiated claim to "indisputable sovereignty" over these islands, this statement raises vitally important legal questions about what, exactly, is meant by "adjacent" and "relevant" waters, over which China also claimed "sovereign rights."

This book will describe the part I played in the attempt to get international legal clarity on these vital and weighty issues, via an appeal to arbitration with reference to UNCLOS – the internationally-recognized UN Convention on the Law of the Sea, which entered into force in November 1994, after more than 14 years of debate and discussion.

Before we move on to describe that process, it is worth exploring the historic origins of China's extraordinary and unprecedented "nine-dash line."

***

Dr Bill Hayton is a former BBC Journalist, an associate fellow with the Asia-Pacific programme at Chatham House and the author of books on China, Vietnam and the South China Sea. We talked about China's "historic claims" in the South China Sea.

"There are plenty of ancient Chinese manuscripts which talk about islands," Hayton said, "but nobody knows really which islands these refer to. At different points in history, whoever was ruling China would be worried about pirates on the coast or smuggling – it's not as if China has been totally land-bound, there has been plenty of engagement with the sea – but often the sea was seen as a place from which danger came. There's the celebrated admiral and diplomat, Zheng He, in the Ming Dynasty in the early 15th century, and he made expeditions as far afield as Arabia, but he was following well-known routes, and he would have avoided the Spratlys and other island groups like the plague because they were terrible hazards that sailors had learned to avoid. Also, Zheng He's expedition was primarily about the projection of Chinese power and the forging of useful trade relationships, and not about making claims for Chinese sovereignty.

"Zheng He is sometimes held up as a kind of permanent fixture – China constantly patrolling its maritime empire – when he is very much the exception, not the rule. Most Chinese emperors wanted to kind of keep control of things, so they generally wanted to keep their people nearby and under observation. A lot of early trading was done by Malays and Indians and Gujaratis and Arabs and others. There is no real history of China systematically exploring the high seas. More to the point, in terms of the Spratlys and the Paracels, it is unthinkable that China would have had any interest in claiming sovereign rights over uninhabited islands. The islands only became of any interest in the early 20th century when people were interested in mining deposits of guano – bird droppings – for fertilizer. But what is far more significant at that time are China's struggles with foreign powers – especially the French and the Japanese – making claims to territories in the South China Sea. At that point the whole issue becomes caught up with avoiding humiliation at the hands of foreign powers. And in 1933, and again after the Second World War, the fate of the islands becomes a genuine popular cause, and it gets connected to an emerging sense of becoming a Chinese nation again after many periods of real turbulence."[30]

Hayton has researched the emergence of the nine-dash line and has written several journal articles on the issue. He argues that the line is not a reflection of genuinely "historic" issues but is an essentially twentieth-century phenomenon that has become embedded in modern Chinese thinking. As a key moment in the development of this modern narrative, he cites, in a 2019 article in the journal *Modern China*, the 1907 occupation of Pratas Island (Chinese: *Dongsha* Island), a coral reef about halfway between China and then-Japanese-ruled Taiwan, by a Japanese entrepreneur who had begun mining guano there. When the imperial Qing-dynasty Chinese Admiral, Li Zhun, arrived at the island in a gunboat in 1909 to investigate, the businessman told him that the island was unoccupied, so he had claimed it for Japan and set up his guano mining business, employing some 100 laborers. When news of the occupation reached mainland China, there was real public concern and outrage. As Hayton notes, "It was after Li's return from Pratas that he and his colleagues […] took the first steps in what would become a decades-long process of constructing a territorial claim to the features of the South China Sea."

Hayton also says that "This appears to be the first moment that Chinese public opinion – or at least some part of it in a few southern port cities – began to take an interest in the sovereignty of the South China Sea." [31] More specifically, Hayton says, this was the first moment at which China had faced the need to address sovereignty issues "within the Western rubric of international law," where it had previously seen the world in terms of Chinese spheres of influence and control, rather than in terms of legal sovereignty. As Hayton writes later in the same article, "There is a conception of territory here that is different from international notions of administrative control. The islands are Chinese by virtue of being near China and visited by Chinese fishermen."

Admiral Li looked for records that would demonstrate China's sovereignty over Pratas Island but could find no historical charts that would back up this claim. As he wrote later in his life, "the territorial sea was not a prime concern in Chinese history. Consequentially, China has neither the nautical charts nor the knowledge of foreign invasion of nearby islands for thousands of years."[32]

Admiral Li eventually found a scholar who had seen a reference to Pratas Island under its Chinese name in an eighteenth-century book, and the Chinese used this in their negotiations with the Japanese. In the end, China paid compensation to the Japanese businessman in order to reclaim *Dongsha* or "East Sands" (Pratas) Island as Chinese territory.

It seems that Li was inspired by this episode to look for other nearby islands that should be seen as belonging to China, because he urged the imperial Qing government to send a ship west to the Paracels (known in China as the *Xisha* or "West Sands" Islands), the location of which he learned from another experienced naval commander. The Chinese government seem to have been vaguely aware of the Paracels. In the 1890s it had been asked for compensation for the loss of two ships that had foundered there and had refused specifically because the Paracels were not then seen as part of the Chinese Empire.[33] But they paid little further attention to them in the subsequent decade. After the discovery of the Japanese on Pratas, a ship was sent to the Paracels in early 1909 and returned with a number of live turtles and reports of deserted islands. Li led a subsequent expedition of three ships back to the Paracels and declared Chinese sovereignty over them in the "Western" manner, firing his ships' canons, hoisting flags and giving the islands Chinese names.[34]

In 1911, the Qing dynasty, founded in 1644, was overthrown following years of uprisings and unrest, leading to the emergence of Chiang Kai-shek's Nationalist movement and the foundation of the Republic of China (ROC).

In the 1930s, the French government – at a time when France was still the colonial power in Indochina – claimed sovereignty over the islands, a claim that China rejected. The ROC was far from being a stable government at the time. Japan had invaded parts of northeastern China in 1931 and consolidated their position, forcing the ROC to recognise *Manchukuo* – "the Empire of Great Manchuria" – a puppet state of the Japanese Empire. Chiang Kai-shek's leadership of the ROC was also challenged by a breakaway regime in China's southwest.

When France announced its annexation of six islands in the Spratlys in 1933, this was seen as a further affront to Chinese nationalism and a sign of the weakness of the ROC government, which was exploited by the breakaway regime. Intriguingly – and amusingly, if the consequences were not so serious – it was generally assumed in China that France had annexed the Paracel Islands, over which France and

China were already in dispute. As Hayton notes, telegrams sent by the Chinese Ministry of Foreign Affairs at the time ask, "Where exactly are these islands? Are they the Paracels?"[35] It took some time for the government to work out that France had annexed an entirely different, more southerly group of islands: the Spratlys.

The ROC decided not to object to France's annexation or to press any claim of its own to the Spratlys. In the face of continued public anger, the ROC Foreign Ministry published an article in its official *Gazette* which was at pains to stress that the islands annexed by France were *not* the Paracel (*Xisha*) Islands, and listing the names of the different islands involved. In a comment next to its listing of Triton (*Nanji* or "southernmost") Island in the Paracels, the article notes that *Nanji* Island was so-called "because it is in the southernmost part of the South China Sea." A previous 1928 Chinese report into commercial activity into guano-mining activities on the Paracels had also stated, "The Paracel archipelago is our nation's southernmost territory."[36] It is clear that, before the 1930s, China had little or no idea as to where or what the Spratly Islands were, and made no territorial claims to them, and saw the Paracels – claimed for China by Admiral Li in 1909 – as the southernmost part of Chinese territory.

All this was to change.

The widespread newspaper coverage of France's annexation of the Spratlys embedded the idea in the public consciousness that the Spratlys had been "stolen" from China, despite the fact that China had never previously claimed any sovereignty over them. In 1935, an ROC geographical body, the Land and Water Maps Review Committee, set about listing all of the features in the South

China Sea and giving them English and Chinese names. Because the committee was not equipped to carry out maritime surveys of its own, it relied predominantly on British maps, and the Chinese names given to features were mostly transliterations of existing English names. Hayton notes that the British map sources can be clearly identified, because several non-existent features, identified in error by earlier British cartographers, were brought over into the new map. The Committee also misunderstood references to two features that are, in fact, permanently underwater banks or shoals, not islands or low-tide elevation reefs: the James Shoal and the Vanguard Bank. A year after the ROC Committee published its map in 1936, a Chinese cartographer, Bai Meichu, who was the founder of the China Geography Society and an ardent nationalist, drew up a new map to include the changes made by the Committee – and made his own, novel addition: a U-shaped line that gathered in all of the features in the South China Sea. Its southernmost point was the (underwater) James Shoal, and its most south-westerly point was the (underwater) Vanguard Bank – both based on the committee's misunderstanding of the features depicted in earlier British maps.

This line marked Bai's (personal) opinion as to the limits of China's territory. It had no status in international maritime law.

Then everything changed again.

In 1937, Japan invaded China, sparking a war that would end with Japan's surrender in 1945 at the end of WWII, after Japan had sided with Nazi Germany and Italy in 1940. During the war, in 1939, Japan seized both the Spratlys and the Paracels and used them as bases. In 1941,

Japan launched attacks on the US (at Pearl Harbor, in Hawaii), the Philippines, Hong Kong, Thailand, Malaya and Singapore. In 1942, Japan invaded Burma and the Dutch East Indies. Manila fell on December 27, 1941, and the Philippines were completely overrun by Japan by May 1942.

After Japan's 1945 surrender, two geographers, both students of the mapmaker Bai Meichu, originator of the "U-shaped line" were charged with creating a new map of the South China Sea – a *Location Sketch Map of the South China Sea Islands* – to show the territories that China (still governed by the ROC at that point) hoped to recover from Japan after its surrender. The map was to be used at a meeting of ROC ministry representatives.

The Canadian historian and policy analyst Chris P. C. Chung uncovered archive records of their meetings. As Chung writes in the Journal *Modern China*, in 2015, "The earliest archival files examined in this article were written in 1946, which marked a continuance of the scramble for the South China Sea islands." Chung mentions the competing claims of France, Japan, and the ROC and says the ROC "was determined to 'reassert' and 'protect' its sovereignty over these islands from foreign 'infringement.'"[37]

Chung continues: "On September 25, 1946, representatives of the Ministry of Foreign Affairs, Ministry of the Interior, Ministry of National Defense, and ROC Navy General Headquarters (NHQ) convened in the Ministry of the Interior to resolve several issues pertaining to the South China Sea islands. The minutes listed each issue and the resolution agreed upon. The first topic, the most significant, determined the scope of what the ROC would claim in the South China Sea." That "scope" was resolved to be "according to the scope shown in the Ministry of the Interior's copy of the Location Sketch Map of the South China Sea Islands."

The 1946 *Location Sketch Map of the South China Sea Islands* features an "eight-dash line", closely following Bai's U-shaped line. The 1946 map is the first official map to show such a line. A map with an eleven-dash line emerged in an ROC map of 1947, with one of the longer dashes west of the Philippines randomly broken into two, and an additional two lines in the Gulf of Tonkin, between Vietnam and China. These two dashes were later removed by the People's Republic of China (PRC) after its defeat of the ROC, as a diplomatic gesture of solidarity with communist North Vietnam, to yield today's equally meaningless nine-dash line.

As Hayton concludes, "a collective Chinese belief in a 'historic claim' to the reefs and rocks [in the South China Sea] emerged in distinct episodes during the first half of the twentieth century, partly in response to perceived threats to the country's sovereignty, but mainly as attempts to shore up a declining nationalist legitimacy."[38]

The PRC's vaunted "nine-dash line", which it portrays as an expression of China's "historic claim" to the South China Sea, arose from deeply confused efforts by its avowed enemy, the previous government of China, the ROC (now Taiwan), to stake a post-WWII claim to territories that Japan had seized during the war. It is hard to imagine a more confused and muddled – and historically recent – chain of events on which to base what are solemnly portrayed by China as its "historic rights" in the

South China Sea – yet China persists in pursuing its claims in deadly earnest.

CHAPTER 3

Recto Bank –The Battle for Oil and Gas

Recto (Reed) Bank is an extraordinary geological feature: a vast underwater plateau rising from the depths of the South China Sea like a submerged mountain with a flat top. It covers 8,866 square kilometers – an area larger than the entire Province of Rizal – and lies just 9 to 45 meters below the surface. This tablemount, as geologists call it, extends roughly 190 kilometers along its northeast-southwest axis and includes smaller formations with names that echo their European discoverers: Nares Bank and Marie Louise Bank. The bank lies in the West Philippine Sea, about 80 to 140 nautical miles northwest of Palawan, well within the Philippines' Economic Exclusion Zone (EEZ). It is situated to the northeast of the main cluster of the Kalayaan Island Group.

On the morning of March 2, 2011, the survey ship MV *Veritas Voyager* was conducting a seismic survey over Recto Bank. The vessel was a sophisticated Singaporean-flagged ship owned by French geophysical company CGG Veritas and chartered by Forum Energy, a UK-based oil and gas exploration company majority-owned by Philippine interests. It was looking for something the Philippines desperately needed: natural gas.

The ship had deployed its "streamers" – fluid-filled cables full of tiny compressed-air "guns". The sound waves from the guns' small explosions travel down through the water beneath them and bounce back off the seabed. Some wavelengths penetrate the seabed and are reflected back by the boundaries between various different layers of rock and sediment beneath. Hydrophones in the streamers collect the returning noise and digitize it for analysis, allowing the creation of high-resolution images of the subsurface that experts can use to spot structures likely to contain accumulated hydrocarbons.

As the *Veritas Voyager* was carrying out its methodical survey, two Chinese Marine Surveillance (CMS) vessels, numbers 71 and 75,[39] accompanied by seven Chinese fishing boats, appeared on the horizon.[40] The CMS vessels "aggressively approached" the *Veritas Voyager*, according to reports, and ordered it to leave, claiming the area was under Chinese jurisdiction.[41] The president of Forum Energy, conscious of the political sensitivity of the operation, was in constant touch with the survey vessel and with the Philippine General overseeing the operation, General Sabban. Forum's president called Sabban, alarmed, telling him about the incident and saying they were pulling their vessel out of the area. Sabban dispatched two unarmed OV-10 spotter planes to the survey vessel, but by the time they reached it, two hours later, the CMS vessels had gone. Sabban then arranged for two of the Philippines' WWII-vintage naval vessels, the minesweeper BRP *Rizal* and the destroyer BRP *Rajah Humabon*, to protect the *Veritas Voyager*. The ageing ships were a sufficient deterrent to keep the CMS vessels away for a further seven days, allowing the *Voyager* to complete that part of its survey but, to this day, no further exploration of the Recto Bank – and no drilling – has been able to take place.[42]

After the incident, the Philippine government sent China a note verbale, saying "The Philippine government views the aggressive actions of the Chinese vessels as a serious violation of Philippine sovereignty and maritime jurisdiction."[43] The Philippines would later describe a conversation that officials had with the Chinese Embassy in the wake of the incident, during which China claimed "indisputable sovereignty over the waters of *Nansha* Islands [Spratly Islands] where Reed Bank [Recto Bank] is situated."[44]

A later, 2016 ruling by the Permanent Court of Arbitration (PCA) of UNCLOS – the implications of which will be discussed in some detail in a later chapter, because they are key to this book's subject matter – ruled that, in fact, Recto Bank is not part of the Spratly Islands. Additionally, none of the features in the Spratly Islands were judged by the court to be actual "islands" entitled to a 200nm EEZ, meaning that even if China were able to establish meaningful sovereignty claims for any part of the Spratly Islands (which it has failed to do) this would not give them any claim over the Recto Bank.

China's act of wanton aggression in preventing the Philippines from surveying their own waters over Recto Bank was not based on any meaningful interpretation of international law. As a 2019 article in *Rappler* stated, "China covets what belongs to the Philippines"[45] – the oil and gas that may lie under the Recto Bank – but it has no legal right to it. In his 2011 State of the Nation address,

Philippine President Benigno Aquino III said, "Our message to the world is clear: What is ours is ours. Setting foot on Recto Bank is no different from setting foot on Recto Avenue." For non-Filipino readers, I should clarify that Recto Avenue is a bustling commercial street in old downtown Manila, famous for its shops, markets, and street vendors selling traditional Filipino snacks.

***

In 2013, a US Energy Information Administration report released data from a United States Geological Survey (USGS), assessing the South China Sea's hydrocarbon potential. The report noted that "USGS assessments estimate anywhere between 0.8 and 5.4 (mean 2.5) billion barrels of oil and between 7.6 and 55.1 (mean 25.5) trillion cubic feet of natural gas in undiscovered resources" in the overall KIG/Spratly Islands territory.[46] Evidence suggested that most of these resources were concentrated in the Recto Bank.

Forum Energy's 2011 surveys – before they were forced to abandon them – had indicated the presence of 3.4 trillion cubic feet of natural gas in just one gas field, known as the Sampaguita field.[47] To put that in context, it is potentially enough gas to power millions of Philippine homes for decades.

Philippine Supreme Court Justice Antonio Carpio understood the stakes better than most. A corporate lawyer by training, Carpio had become increasingly consumed by the South China Sea dispute after the 2011 Recto Bank incident. He would go on to deliver more than 200 lectures on the issue and write an e-book about disputes in the

South China Sea and the West Philippine Sea.[48] His most urgent message was about energy security.

"Malampaya will run out of gas in 10 years," Carpio warned repeatedly in speeches and interviews, referring to the Malampaya gas field that supplies most of the Philippines' natural gas. "There is urgency to develop Reed Bank as a replacement for the rapidly depleting Malampaya; otherwise, there will be 10 to 12 hours of brownouts every day in Luzon 10 years hence."[49] (A "brownout" refers to an emergency reduction in the voltage of the electrical supply, causing lights to dim and appliances to work on low power, rather than creating a complete "blackout".)

The Philippines are currently almost entirely dependent on imports of crude oil from the Middle East and on the outputs of liquid petroleum products from other Asian countries' refineries, which are themselves dependent on crude oil from that region. At the time of writing (April 2026), the war between the US, Israel and Iran has led to the near closure of the Straits of Hormuz, severely curtailing the export of crude oil. The Philippines experienced the world's steepest rise in fuel prices as a result and was the first country to declare a national energy emergency. The crisis brought into sharp focus the country's reliance on energy imports and the urgent need to develop its own energy resources and improve its energy security.

The Malampaya natural gas field, located 80 kilometers northwest of Palawan in much deeper water than Recto Bank, had been the Philippines' economic lifeline since commercial production began in January 2002. Four power plants, with a combined capacity of 3,200 megawatts, depended on Malampaya gas. When Carpio issued his warning, the field was supplying 20 to 40 percent of Luzon's electricity – including Metro Manila's – but production had been declining for years and the field was approaching depletion. Energy officials spoke hopefully of extending its life into the early 2030s, but everyone knew the truth: Malampaya's days were numbered.

Recto Bank was the obvious replacement. It was closer to shore than Malampaya, in much shallower waters, which would make extraction significantly cheaper. The geological surveys looked promising. Forum Energy held Service Contract 72, awarded by the Philippine Department of Energy. Everything was in place – except that China had made it impossible to proceed.

The Philippines had few alternatives. The country's oil production told a story of fleeting promise. Nido field, discovered in 1977 off northwest Palawan, began producing in February 1979 – the first commercial oil production in Philippine history. It was a moment of hope, but after 40 years, Nido was depleted and it shut down in 2019. Matinloc field, discovered two years after Nido, followed the same trajectory, and also closed the 2019. The Philippine Department of Energy held a ceremony to mark the closure – a polite funeral for the country's oil independence.

By 2020, the Philippines had only three active energy-producing fields: Malampaya for gas, and the small Galoc and Alegria fields for oil. Other discoveries had either been depleted or were no longer commercially viable.[50] Unable to access Recto Bank, the Philippines had no choice but to turn to imported liquefied natural gas. In 2023, two LNG terminals opened in Batangas Bay, with four more planned by 2026. By 2050, government projections estimated LNG imports would reach 24.3 million tonnes of oil-equivalent per annum. The cost of the imports would be enormous – far higher than the cost of developing domestic reserves.

The March 2011 harassment of the *Veritas Voyager* on Recto Bank by two CMS vessels was not an isolated incident; it was a statement of China's intent for the South China Sea as a whole. In May 2011, only a few months later, a Vietnamese seismic exploration ship owned by a joint venture between CGG Veritas and PetroVietnam was exploring Vietnamese waters some 65nm off the country's coast, when CMS ship number 84 deliberately sailed across its streamers, severing them. Weeks later, another CGG Veritas exploration ship, owned by a joint Vietnamese/Canadian venture, was attacked in waters at the southeastern edge of Vietnam's EEZ. This time, the attack came not from CMS vessels, but by ships from China's Fisheries Law Enforcement Command (FLEC), working in conjunction with a small flotilla of Chinese fishing vessels. As the FLEC vessels sailed in front of the exploration vessel, a Chinese trawler sailed across its stern, snagging its nets on the exploration ship's streamers. Other Chinese fishing vessels rushed in to cut the streamers and "rescue" the trawler. There would be other incidents involving Vietnamese and Malaysian exploration vessels in 2012 and 2013.

Describing these incidents in his book *The South China Sea: The Struggle for Power in Asia,* Bill Hayton concludes, "[the incidents] provided yet more evidence that parts of the Chinese state – the China National Offshore Oil Company, China Marine Surveillance and the Fisheries Law Enforcement Command – regarded the 'U-shaped line' as a real claim to 80 percent of the South China Sea.

All the incidents took place far from any Chinese-claimed land feature and therefore seemed incompatible with any claim based on UNCLOS."[51]

A Filipino vessel suffered another attack on Recto Bank in 2019. In June of that year, a wooden-hulled Filipino fishing boat, F/B *Gem-Ver 1*, was anchored at Recto Bank when a Chinese steel-hulled vessel rammed it shortly after midnight and then sailed away, abandoning the twenty-two Filipino crew members. They floated on the wreckage for more than six hours before a Vietnamese fishing vessel rescued them.

The captain of *Gem-Ver 1* told reporters what happened. The Chinese vessel had approached with its lights off, nearly invisible in the darkness. *The Gem-Ver 1* was anchored – stationary, visible, with navigation lights showing and radar reflector deployed. The weather was fair, the sea calm, with a crescent moon and stars overhead. The Chinese vessel smashed into the stern of the fishing boat, spinning it around. Water immediately began to fill the hull. After the ramming, the Chinese vessel turned around and suddenly switched on its powerful lights, shining them on the already sinking boat and the frantic fishermen. "We were blinded by the overpowering light," said one crew member, "there were just so many." The crew of the fishing vessel shouted for help and waved at the Chinese ship. It seemed they were about to be rescued, but the Chinese ship abruptly turned its lights off again and sailed away, leaving them clinging to the wreckage of their sinking boat. "We thought they were going to rescue us," said another of the crew, "but they left us instead."[52]

The Armed Forces of the Philippines concluded the ramming was deliberate. Supreme Court Justice Carpio argued that the vessel was likely part of China's Maritime Militia – civilian fishing boats with reinforced steel hulls designed specifically for ramming, operating under the command of the People's Liberation Army. "Captains of ordinary Chinese fishing vessels do not engage in ramming for fear of inflicting damage to their own vessels," Carpio noted. "It is highly likely that a Chinese maritime militia vessel rammed the Filipino fishing vessel."[53] Philippine Defense Secretary Delfin Lorenzana condemned what he called "the cowardly action of the Chinese fishing vessel and its crew for abandoning the Filipino crew. This is not the expected action from a responsible and friendly people."[54] But China's Foreign Ministry dismissed the incident as "an ordinary maritime traffic accident," and a spokesperson accused the Philippines of politicizing the incident without proof. Philippine Navy Vice-Admiral Robert Emperdrad demurred. "The Filipino boat was anchored," he responded. "Based on the international rules of the road, it had the privilege because it could not evade an incoming ship. So the boat was rammed. This is not a normal incident."[55]

In August – two months after the sinking of the Filipino vessel – the owner of the Chinese vessel issued an apology. As a senator, I issued a statement pointing out that the apology finally confirmed the correctness of the Philippine's account of the incident, despite China's dismissals and denials. "The apology coming from the Chinese side, while two months late, shows the validity of the Philippine version of the incident," my statement said. I went on to press for civil damages and to promise to continue to work towards further legal protections for Filipino fishermen: "We should pursue our civil claim for damages to give justice to our fishermen as well as seek other routes to protect them in the future hand in hand with our sovereign rights."[56]

The history of attempted joint energy exploration and development in Recto Bank reads like a case study in diplomatic futility. China's approach has always been straightforward, even if it is legally and morally unjustifiable. China argues that the South China Sea "indisputably" belongs to China because of its unprovable "historic claims", but it is willing to enter into dialogue about joint development of oil and gas resources. In 2005, the Philippines had entered the Joint Marine Seismic Undertaking (JMSU) – a tripartite agreement with China and Vietnam to conduct surveys in a massive 142,886-square-kilometer area of the South China Sea, about 80 percent of which lay within the Philippine EEZ.

The agreement was surrounded by controversy from the start. Critics accused the administration of Philippine president Gloria Macapagal Arroyo of secrecy and of selling out Philippine sovereignty. The agreement was linked to a larger $904 million Chinese investment package, raising questions about whether the Philippines had traded away its maritime rights for infrastructure funding.[57] More fundamentally, such an agreement was in likely breach of the Constitution of the Philippines, which demanded a 60% Filipino shareholding for all companies involved in natural resource exploration.

The JSMU's surveys were completed in 2007, but the results China shared with the Philippines were not made public. "We have been trying to follow up the results of the survey," wrote veteran journalist and *VERA Files* president Ellen T. Tordesillas in 2017, "but we were told that what the Chinese shared with the Philippines was 'hazy'."[58] The agreement expired in 2008.

In November 2018, President Duterte's administration reopened the idea of joint development by signing a Memorandum of Understanding (MOU) with China for joint oil and gas exploration. The MOU set out to create a framework to create "cooperation agreements" via a steering committee and working groups "without prejudice to the respective legal positions of both governments" and which did "not create rights or obligations under international or domestic law ."[59] One idea that surfaced under the MOU was that the China National Offshore Oil Corporation (CNOOC) could become a "service provider" for the Philippine government. The hypothetical deal was structured so that 60 percent of the proceeds would go to the Philippine government, as owner of the resources, via the Philippine's PXP Energy Group, who would employ CNOOC for its services and technology in return for 40 percent of proceeds. It was a clever solution that retained the principle of Philippine ownership of its own resources while allowing China to benefit from the deal but, as a former Philippine Department of Energy official told *BenarNews* in 2023, as reported by Radio Free Asia, "Beijing rejected it because it would have been tantamount to acknowledging Philippine sovereignty in the area."[60] The Philippine government reimposed a moratorium on exploration in April 2022.

In January 2023, after a petition that had languished for nearly 15 years, the Philippine Supreme Court finally ruled on the constitutional issue at the heart of the JMSU – the tripartite agreement between the Philippines, China and Vietnam on the joint seismic exploration of huge areas of the South China Sea – and, by implication, on any other agreement involving other nations. The Court's decision was unequivocal. By a vote of 12-2-1, it declared the tripartite deal unconstitutional. The agreement had violated Article XII, Section 2 of the 1987 Constitution, which reserves exploration of Philippine natural resources to Filipino citizens or corporations that are at least 60 percent Filipino-owned. The Chinese and Vietnamese state oil companies – the CNOOC and PetroVietnam – were wholly foreign-owned. The government had argued that the JMSU was merely "pre-exploration," not actual exploration. The Supreme Court dismissed this distinction entirely. "Exploration pertains to a search or discovery of something in both its ordinary or technical sense," the Court ruled. Calling it "pre-exploration" didn't change what it was.[61] The ruling was crystal clear: only Filipinos or Filipino-controlled corporations had the constitutional right to conduct explorations for the Philippine's natural resources. Any form of "joint deal" with other nations was unconstitutional.

When President Ferdinand Marcos Jr. took office, he lifted the moratorium again in 2025 in the hope of further exploration and development by Forum Energy, whose contract was still valid, though suspended, or any other interest contractor. A Philippine Navy spokesman announced that naval forces would do what they could to protect Recto Bank if, or when, exploration resumed. But at the time of writing, Recto Bank remains unexploited, its vast reserves locked beneath the seabed.

Recto Bank has become more than an energy issue. It has become a symbol of everything that is at stake in the South China Sea: a nation's sovereign rights under international law versus the reality of power; economic necessity versus geopolitical impossibility; paper victories versus facts on the water; might versus right.

Justice Carpio's warning about 10 to 12 hours of daily brownouts in Luzon may yet come to pass – not because the Philippines lacks energy resources in its own waters, but because it cannot access them. The gas beneath Recto Bank could power homes, fuel industries, generate billions in revenue. Instead, it remains trapped beneath the seabed, guarded by Chinese vessels, claimed by Chinese maps with their crude nine dashes, subject to Chinese "indisputable sovereignty" pronounced over waters that have never belonged to China and never will under any rational interpretation of international law.

If the lights eventually dim across Luzon, Recto Bank will stand as a monument to the gap between law and power, between rights and reality, between what the Philippines owns and what it can actually use.

This is why the fight for the West Philippine Sea matters. This is why the battle to enshrine the 2016 arbitral ruling in Philippine law became so critical. And this is why China was so determined to stop it – and to punish those of us, like me, who tried.

CHAPTER 4

The Standoff at Panatag Shoal

On the morning of April 8, 2012, a Philippine Air Force surveillance plane circled over Panatag (Scarborough) Shoal, (also known as Bajo de Masinloc), a triangular chain of reefs and rocks about 120 nautical miles west of Luzon, well within the Philippine's Economic Exclusion Zone (EEZ). The pilots radioed back troubling news: eight Chinese fishing vessels lay anchored in the shoal's lagoon, which Filipino and other nation's fishermen had used for decades as shelter from typhoons, while the waters in and around the shoal provided rich fishing grounds. President Benigno Aquino III ordered an immediate response. The Philippine Navy deployed its largest naval frigate, the BRP *Gregorio del Pilar* – a recently acquired Hamilton-class cutter that had been gifted to the Philippines by the United States after being decommissioned from the US Coast Guard – to enforce the country's fisheries and environmental protection laws.

What happened next would transform the dispute about China's "historic claim" to the South China Sea. What quickly became a standoff at Panatag Shoal would expose the limits of American security guarantees to the

Philippines, demonstrate China's willingness to use economic coercion against smaller neighbors in addition to physical occupation and denial of access, and ultimately convince Manila that bilateral negotiations with Beijing were futile. The final loss of the shoal to Chinese blunt force and the failure of efforts to find a diplomatic resolution would set the Philippines on a path it had long avoided but which now seemed to be the only option: international arbitration.

Panatag Shoal is a large coral atoll, about 10 miles across at its widest point, with a narrow entrance at one corner. At high tide, the reef is simply an array of rocks poking out of the sea. Inside the reef, the waters are relatively shallow: from 9 to 13 meters deep, and as little as 1.7 meters in some patches. The feature appears on a famous 1734 map of the Philippine archipelago as "Panacot" – the Tagalog word for "danger" or "threat," as mentioned earlier. The map was made by a Spanish Jesuit, Murillo Velarde, and is often referred to as "the Mother of All Philippine Maps."

The coral reefs of the South China Sea are incredibly rich and important ecosystems. As Professor Jay Batonbacal, director of the University of the Philippines Institute for Maritime Affairs and the Law of the Sea, highlighted in a lecture on the history and significance of Bajo de Masinloc, scientific research has confirmed the importance of the reef as "an offshore shelter, regeneration area, migration path, and food supply for the fisheries in, as well as around, the South China Sea." [62] In his lecture, Batongbacal shows satellite imagery of the concentration of chlorophyll in different areas of the South China Sea. A plume of chlorophyll can be seen connecting Bajo de

Masinloc to the Philippine Archipelago. “Chlorophyll represents plankton,” says Batongbacal, “the base of the marine food chain; where the plankton go, the fish follow.” Bajo de Masinloc is a hugely important part of the food chain of the West Philippine Sea, offering a breeding ground for many species whose progeny then disperse through the region.

The presence of Chinese fishing vessels at Bajo de Masinloc was not in itself alarming or unusual – Filipino fishermen had traditionally shared the shoal with fishermen from China, Vietnam and Taiwan. But the presence of eight Chinese trawlers inside the shoal suggested a more industrial scale of fishing than typical artisanal fishing, and the main concern was whether the ships were illegally harvesting protected species.

The BRP *Gregorio del Pilar* arrived at Scarborough on April 10, 2012. Armed sailors boarded the Chinese vessels one by one, conducting what naval officers call VBSS operations – visit, board, search, and seizure. Inside the first fishing boat, they discovered what one report described as "large amounts of illegally collected corals, giant clams and live sharks."[63] The Filipino inspection team prepared to arrest the fishermen for violations of Philippine law and of the International Convention on International Trade in Endangered Species.

Very soon afterwards, two Chinese Marine Surveillance (CMS) ships, CMS 75 and 84, appeared over the horizon and sailed directly to the mouth of the lagoon, positioning themselves between the Philippine frigate and the Chinese fishing vessels. The Philippine Navy's attempt to make arrests was blocked. A standoff had begun.

For the Aquino administration, this posed an immediate dilemma. China immediately portrayed the BRP *Gregorio del Pilar*'s presence as a dangerous escalation of the dispute – Manila had chosen to send a "warship" (naval vessel) rather than a "lawship" (coastguard vessel) to deal with a fisheries dispute. The *Gregorio del Pilar* was also not just any warship, but a former US coastguard vessel that had donated to the Philippines in 2011 by the US as part of a trend of growing cooperation between the two nations, a trend that was confirmed in the fall of that year by US President Obama's announcement of a "Pivot to Asia" in a speech to the Australian parliament in November of that year. On April 12, 2012, President Aquino ordered the withdrawal of the *Gregorio del Pilar.* A smaller Philippine Coast Guard (PCG) vessel, BRP *Pampanga*, would take its place to maintain a Philippine presence, sharing its duties over time with BRP *Edsa II*. But, to some extent, the damage was done. China had successfully reframed the confrontation as uncalled-for Philippine "militarization" of a dispute about illegal fishing. A third Chinese vessel soon arrived at the shoal.

The incident that led to the 2012 standoff did not come "out of the blue" nor was it unprecedented. In her book, *Rock Solid: How the Philippines Won Its Maritime Case against China*, Filipino author and journalist Marites Dañguilan Vitug recounts a long litany of incidents between the Philippine Navy and Chinese vessels at Bajo de Masinloc stretching back to the 1990s. Chinese fishermen had been found catching protected species such as sea turtles, fishing using prohibited techniques such as the use of dynamite and cyanide, and illegally harvesting coral. Chinese fishing boats were apprehended and searched; crews were sometimes charged under Philippine law. In 2000, three Chinese boats were boarded in Bajo de Masinloc and found to be carrying what Vitug describes as "tons of corals, more than fifty blasting caps, more than a hundred dynamite strips, at least dozen bottles of cyanide and a 32-foot detonating cord."[64] One ship was impounded and towed back to the Philippines, but the other vessels escaped that night under cover of darkness. The impounded Chinese ship was later released. Such incidents led to a constant stream of protests from China, followed by diligent Philippine explanations about the illegality of Chinese fishermen's activities – and no apparent change in Chinese behavior. As Vitug describes it: "The back-and-forth memos between the Philippine embassy in Beijing and the DFA [Department of Foreign Affairs] in Manila showed a pattern of protest, dialogue, and a repetition of the unlawful acts. It was a cycle that played itself out with China adamant on its declared 'indisputable sovereignty' over the shoal."

In the days after the initial event, Philippine Foreign Secretary, Albert del Rosario, worked to find a diplomatic solution. He met repeatedly with Chinese Ambassador, Ma Keqing. On April 13, 2012, a brief breakthrough seemed possible. Following talks between Del Rosario and Ma, two Chinese cutters escorted the Chinese fishing boats out of the shoal, leaving Manila and Beijing with one ship each at the atoll. The optimism lasted only a few hours. That same evening, negotiations collapsed. Del Rosario had been insistent that the fishermen should not leave with their illegal catch intact; the Chinese ambassador demanded that the Philippines withdraw its final remaining vessel before China withdrew its own. The following morning, Del Rosario declared a "stalemate". A second Chinese vessel returned to the shoal.[65]

On April 17, 2012, Del Rosario proposed that the Philippines and China should take the dispute to the UN International Tribunal for the Law of the Sea. China rejected the proposal, saying the issue should be resolved "through friendly consultations so as not to complicate or aggravate the incident."[66] The Philippine government also appealed to the Association of Southeast Asian Nations (ASEAN) to "take a stand." Beijing immediately rejected these attempts to "internationalize" the crisis,[67] maintaining its usual interest in reaching bilateral agreements with nations it was in dispute with – a continuation of China's "take and talk" strategy: seizing control of a feature in the South China Sea and then suggesting that some sort of reasonable accommodation can be made with the feature's "rightful owner", China.

On April 28, 2012, a Chinese Fisheries Law Enforcement Command (FLEC) vessel, FLEC-310, carried out a series of dangerous and intimidating maneuvers outside the shoal, approaching the *Pampanga* at high speed before veering away at the last moment, and carrying out the same maneuver with the *Edsa II*, which was also at the shoal at the time. Sometime later, a team from the Philippine's Bureau of Fisheries and Aquatic Resources (BFAR) joined the PCG vessels. They boarded a small rubber boat and were able to enter the shoal, where they witnessed Chinese boats towing something on a rope through the waters inside the shoal – presumably some kind of dredger or trawl net – causing much discoloration of the waters. On a second occasion, the BFAR team took underwater video showing destruction of coral inside the reef and saw illegally harvested giant clams inside some of the Chinese vessels.[68] By May 21, 2012, China had deployed five Chinese cutters and over a dozen fishing trawlers to the shoal.[69]

On May 26, 2012, a BFAR ship taking supplies to Coastguard vessels at the shoal faced dangerous harassment by both CMS and FLEC. As they tried to enter the shoal, they found their way blocked by several Chinese vessels moored at the shoal's entrance and were forced to back away to avoid getting entangled with the vessels' mooring ropes. They eventually managed to enter the shoal, despite last-minute efforts by a FLEC vessel which, according to their report, went "all engines back and attempted to ram our vessel. Still, we continued to employ speed and immediately maneuvered hard left just enough to dodge from the deliberate intention of the FLEC." A little later, a Philippine Islander reconnaissance plane saw that some 28 Chinese vessels had been roped together across the entrance to the shoal to prevent the entry of any more Philippine vessels.[70] The Philippine vessels trapped inside were later allowed to leave, but any further re-entry was blocked.[71]

Also in May 2012, the standoff took a new, economic twist. Following peaceful spontaneous demonstrations by Filipinos outside the Chinese consular office in Manila, protesting against China's continuing occupation of Panatag Shoal, Beijing again reacted aggressively, accusing the Philippines of escalating tensions by fomenting unrest. Then it was discovered that Chinese authorities were refusing entry to Chinese ports of some 1500 containers of bananas exported from the Philippines. The president of the Philippine's main banana growers' and exporters' association, Stephen Antig, announced that the containers were being denied entry at various Chinese ports and were being held without any power supply for their refrigeration units, meaning the fruit would soon rot. "The bananas are being held in the ports for inspection," Antig told reporters, "when in just a matter of three days, the bananas can turn into vinegar." Chinese authorities said that the heightened level of "inspection" was required because of the earlier discovery of an invasive and harmful scale insect in a shipment of Philippine bananas, leading to the new inspection regime. One problem with this version of accounts was that the scale insect pest that China claimed to have found earlier occurs only in coconuts, not bananas. China is a major market for Philippine bananas. Antig said that since the new rules had been enforced, Filipino banana exporters had lost around 1 billion Philippine pesos – around US$17 million.[72]

The next weapon in China's economic arsenal was tourism, with the announcement of travel restrictions from China to the Philippines. The Philippines' most important markets for tourism were Korea, the US and Japan, with China the fourth most significant market. There had been over 96,000 visits from China in 2011, a 77% increase over the previous year, according to *The Philippine Daily Inquirer*, reporting figures from the Department of Tourism. [73] Tourism-related stocks on the Philippine stock market fell. The *Inquirer* said that "the latest Chinese move amounted to an economic boycott as a weapon of nonviolent retaliation."

At the end of April 2012, Foreign Secretary Del Rosario and Defense Secretary Voltaire Gazmin had met with their US counterparts, Secretary of State Hilary Clinton and Defense Secretary Leon E. Panetta. "We oppose the threat or use of force by any party to advance its claim," Clinton said after the meeting in Washington, referring to China's occupation of the shoal, "and we will remain in close contact with our ally, the Philippines." Asked if the US would come to the Philippines' aid if the country was attacked by China during the standoff, Del Rosario replied, "They have expressed that they will honor their obligations under the mutual defense treaty."[74] The US, however, remained keen to de-escalate the situation. *The Financial Time*s reported that in June, Kurt Campbell, the US Assistant Secretary of State for East Asian and Pacific Affairs had taken advantage of a visit to Washington by Fu Ying, China's Vice Foreign Minister for Asia and a former Ambassador to the Philippines, to arrange a meeting in a Virginia Hotel.[75] According to *VERA Files*, both the Philippine DFA and Chinese sources said that Campbell had proposed a simultaneous withdrawal of both Chinese and Philippine vessels from Bajo de Masinloc. The US seemed to believe that the proposal had been accepted and that such an agreement had been made. Harry Taylor, the US Ambassador to the Philippines, put in a call to Del Rosario to tell him that China had agreed to a joint withdrawal.[76] Del Rosario ordered the two remaining Philippine vessels to leave Bajo de Masinloc.[77] The following morning, it was discovered the Chinese vessels had remained in place. A later statement by the Philippine DFA said, "the Philippines forged an agreement with a neighboring country for the simultaneous pullout of all vessels inside the shoal, which we undertook in good faith (…) Yet to this day, the neighboring country has not fulfilled its obligations under the agreement and has maintained its ships inside and outside the shoal, as well as its barrier, in its aim to establish effective control and jurisdiction in the shoal and surrounding waters."[78]

It seems likely that the US had overestimated the strength of the "agreement" they felt they had made with China's Fu Ying. Citing Chinese sources, *VERA Files* reported that Fu had promised only to relay the suggestion to Beijing. The source said that a "gradual pullout" had been envisaged and "there was never a commitment for a total pullout," because China "have a domestic audience to consider" – a complete pullout would be seen as a climbdown and a loss of face. The news organization also reported that President Aquino was unhappy that Del Rosario had ordered the Philippine vessels to withdraw. Aquino had set up a "back channel" to Beijing, using Senator Antonio Trillanes IV, who had many meetings with Fu and was reportedly taking a more conciliatory approach to China.[79] China sent word via Trillanes that they would issue a statement about recalling their ships and asked for 48 hours to inform the appropriate agencies. But then, according to *VERA Files*, Beijing was apparently "angered" by the DFA statement accusing China of reneging on the agreement that China denied having made.

Whatever the truth of these matters, the end result was that Chinese vessels never left Bajo de Masinloc, where they never had any business to "set up camp" in the first place. China remains in illegal possession of the shoal to this day.

When ASEAN foreign ministers gathered in Cambodia in July, China pressured the host country to keep the South China Sea dispute off the agenda. According to Dr Ely Ratner, US Assistant Secretary of Defense for Asia-Pacific Security, writing in *The National Interest*, "Chinese President Hu Jintao visited Phnom Penh prior to the summit with promises of millions of dollars in investment and assistance. This was enough to convince Cambodia to limit discussions on sensitive maritime issues that would have highlighted China's assertiveness." The resulting discord prevented ASEAN from issuing a joint communiqué for the first time in its 45-year history.[80] For the Philippines, appealing for international arbitration began to seem the only route forward.

Within President Aquino's cabinet, a fierce debate about international arbitration had been underway since the standoff began. I was a member of the Cabinet at that time, as Chairman of the MMDA. Some officials feared that pursuing international arbitration would further damage relations with Beijing and might provoke even harsher Chinese retaliation. Another faction, led by Foreign Secretary del Rosario, argued that the Philippines had exhausted every diplomatic avenue. Bilateral talks had produced nothing but humiliation; ASEAN had proven toothless in the face of Chinese pressure. The US-brokered withdrawal deal – if it ever truly existed in China's eyes – had failed. The loss of Bajo de Masinloc, coming on top of China's earlier seizure of Mischief Reef in 1994 and its subsequent development into an "artificial island," proved that Beijing would simply take what it wanted unless legally challenged.

Justice Carpio, in particular, championed the idea that international law offered the Philippines a way to compete in a forum where it had advantages. In a 2020 speech he had given on his acceptance of a honorary doctoral degree from the University of the Philippines, Carpio recalled his horror when China had seized Mischief Reef, at a time when he was Chief Presidential Legal Counsel to President Fidel Ramos. "The Philippines was totally defenseless," said Carpio. "We did not have the military capability to take back Mischief Reef. (…) This incident left a deep scar in my mind – that a powerful state could just grab what legally belonged to a weaker state, and there was no power on earth that could right such a wrong."[81]

At the end of the speech, Carpio harked back to what he had written in 2010 – two years before the Bajo de Masinloc standoff – when he first began his mission to find a legal basis for defending the Philippine's EEZ in the West Philippine Sea. *"This battle to defend our EEZ from China, the superpower in our region, is the 21st century equivalent of the battles that our forebears waged against Western and Eastern colonizers from the 16th to the 20th century. The best and the brightest of our forebears fought the Western and Eastern colonizers, and even sacrificed their lives, to make the Philippines free.*

"In this modern day battle, the best and the brightest legal warriors in our country today must stand up and fight to free the EEZ of the Philippines from foreign encroachment. In this historic battle to secure our EEZ, we must rely on the most powerful weapon invented by man in the settlement of disputes among states – a weapon that can immobilize armies, neutralize aircraft carriers, render irrelevant nuclear bombs, and level the battlefield between small nations and superpowers.

"That weapon – the great equalizer – is the Rule of Law. Under the Rule of Law, right prevails over might."

The country could never match China ship-for-ship or dollar-for-dollar. But in an arbitration tribunal under the United Nations Convention on the Law of the Sea (UNCLOS), the Philippines could present legal arguments on an equal footing with Beijing. The evidence was on Manila's side: Bajo de Masinloc lay well within the Philippines' EEZ. Under UNCLOS – which China had finally ratified in 1996, having signed it in 1982 when it first opened for signature – the shoal could not possibly belong to Beijing, unless it were able to provide the court with some meaningful basis for its sweeping "historical claims" to sovereignty.

For Aquino, the Bajo de Masinloc standoff tipped the balance. The pattern was now undeniable: China was incrementally seizing Philippine territory, using its superior military and economic power, and then daring Manila to do something about it. By January 2013, the "cold standoff"" at Bajo de Masinloc had become China's effective occupation.

On January 22, 2013, the Philippines formally initiated arbitration proceedings under UNCLOS. The case would take three and a half years to wind through the Permanent Court of Arbitration in The Hague, but its outcome would reshape the legal landscape of the South China Sea dispute.

CHAPTER 5

The Constitution of the Oceans

For centuries, "the freedom of the seas" had been accepted as a fact of seafaring life. Fishermen fished wherever they could find fish, with no sense that the fish "belonged" to anyone. Mariners sailed to wherever they were able and could land and disembark at will on coastlines that were not well defended. More powerful nations with coastal defenses and strong navies could deter adventurers and repel invaders; other countries were open to occasional raids from the sea or to full-scale invasion by more powerful colonizing forces.

The Dutch lawyer and statesman, Hugo Grotius, writing in the first half of the seventeenth century, was a strong advocate of the freedom of the seas – which suited his home country's position as a great naval and trading (and colonialist) power. He argued that the sea belonged to everyone and that any nation could only claim sovereign rights over the narrow stretch of water off its coast that it was able to physically defend and control.

In the early eighteenth century, another Dutch legalist called Cornelius van Bynkershoek argued that the width of that stretch of territorial sea was dictated by the range of the coastal state's defensive weapons – in those days, cannons. An Italian called Ferdinando Galiani calculated that the range of the most advanced cannons of the time was three nautical miles (nm) – though, in fact, most cannons' effective range was considerably less. But 3nm also happened to be the equivalent of the widely used nautical unit of distance, the league, and the idea that nations had a sovereign right to the waters up to 3nm, or one league, from their coast became commonly known as the "cannon-shot rule." By the mid-twentieth century, this ancient doctrine was collapsing as defensive weapons became hugely more powerful and nations' competing interests became more fraught.

In 1945, President Harry Truman unilaterally extended the United States' control over all natural resources on its continental shelf and in the waters above them, to protect US fisheries from foreign fishing fleets and with an eye to the future exploitation of oil and mineral resources below the seabed of the country's continental shelf. In the meantime, the US was itself engaged – along with Japan and the USSR – in extensive distant-water fishing, off the coast of West Africa and in the Eastern Pacific in particular. This was perfectly legal, provided the foreign fishing fleets were operating outside the coastal nations' 3nm territorial waters, but there was growing concern among developing nations that the more powerful, developed nations were harvesting resources they should at least have first claim to. Between 1946 and 1950, Chile, Peru, and Ecuador had claimed rights extending 200nm from their coasts to protect their rich fishing grounds – waters fueled by the Humboldt Current: a cold, nutrient-rich, north-flowing body of water that supports huge populations of fish and other marine life. There was a growing sense that the ancient concept of relatively narrow territorial waters and "the high seas" – which, in effect, were controlled and exploited by the nations that had the most powerful navies and the most technologically-advanced fishing fleets – was no longer a viable global order.

The United Nations attempted to address these issues in 1958 at the first Conference on the Law of the Sea (UNCLOS), held in Geneva. The conference resulted in four separate conventions, covering territorial seas, continental shelves, the high seas and fishing rights, but failed to resolve the issue of how far nations' territorial waters should extend. A second conference in 1960 failed entirely to reach agreement on this issue. The developing world found itself largely sidelined in these early negotiations, with little meaningful voice in decisions that would profoundly affect their futures.

On November 1, 1967, a speech given by Arvid Pardo, the Maltese Ambassador to the General Assembly of the United Nations, would have a profound effect on the development of future maritime law. Malta was among the smallest members of the UN, yet Pardo was about to make one of the most consequential proposals in the history of international maritime law – one which would earn him the title, "Father of the Law of the Sea."

Pardo's main concern was with the deep ocean floor beyond nations' continental shelves and outside any national jurisdiction. In the 1970s, corporations and governments were actively exploring the commercial viability of deep-sea mining, particularly for manganese nodules – potato-sized deposits containing manganese, cobalt, nickel and copper that carpet substantial areas of the deep ocean floor and seemed to offer rich pickings for anyone with the ability to collect them (to date, commercial mining of these nodules has never been undertaken). The potential to "militarize" the seabed through the installation of remotely controlled undersea weapons systems was also increasingly obvious.

As Pardo said in his speech, "The known resources of the sea-bed and of the ocean floor are far greater than the resources known to exist on dry land. The sea-bed and the ocean floor are also of vital and increasing strategic importance. Present and clearly foreseeable technology also permits their effective exploitation for military or economic purposes. Some countries may therefore be tempted to use their technological competence to achieve near-unbreakable world dominance through predominant control over the sea-bed and the ocean floor." This, Pardo thought, could "lead to a competitive scramble for sovereign rights over the land underlying the world's seas and oceans, surpassing in magnitude and in its implications last century's colonial scramble for territory in Asia and Africa."[82]

Pardo proposed that the seabed beyond national jurisdictions should be declared the "common heritage of mankind" – a concept that would eventually find its way into the UNCLOS. He argued that some of the sea's wealth should be used to help close the gap between rich and poor nations, and that the international community needed to act before unilateral claims and private exploitation carved up the ocean floor among the most technologically advanced nations. Part of Pardo's concern was that a 1958 Continental Shelf Convention had defined the continental shelf as "the seabed and subsoil of the submarine areas adjacent to the coast but outside the area of the territorial sea, to a depth of 200 meters or, beyond that limit, to where the depth of the superjacent waters admits of the exploitation of the natural resources."[83] This had the effect of defining a continental shelf in terms of the depth to which it was technologically feasible to exploit resources – a definition that was susceptible to "technological creep", as developed nations found ways of exploring and extracting resources at ever-greater ocean depths.

Pardo's speech struck a chord. In the late 1960s, the Cold War between the US and the Soviet Union and their respective allies was at its height, with both superpowers looking for ways to gain a decisive military advantage, and with the high seas and deep oceans being very much part of that global battlefield. Developing nations, many newly independent, were demanding a greater voice in global affairs and a fairer share of the world's resources. The environmental movement was gathering strength. Technological advances were making it possible to potentially exploit resources in ever-deeper waters and to use the oceans in ways that had previously been unimaginable. The time was ripe to try to find a modern approach to a legal framework that had barely evolved since medieval times.

In 1973, the third UNCLOS convened in New York, beginning a negotiation process that would last nearly a decade and would eventually produce what is now universally accepted as "the Constitution of the Sea".

***

The Philippines played a crucial role in UNCLOS III, and at the forefront of the Philippine delegation was Senator Arturo Tolentino. Senator Tolentino was widely regarded as one of the greatest legal minds of his time – a constitutionalist whose intellect and discipline helped shape the foundations of Philippine law. To his students, young lawyers and colleagues, he was more than an academician. He was both a "lolo" and grandfather of the legal profession, a steady and guiding presence whose wisdom was generously shared and deeply felt. In him, many found not only a teacher of law, but a source of counsel, character and continuity – an enduring figure whose legacy lives on in the generations he mentored and inspired.

Born in Manila in 1910, Senator Arturo Tolentino was already one of the Philippines' most distinguished legal minds when he took on the challenge of representing his nation's maritime interests at the United Nations. A graduate of the University of the Philippines College of Law, where his academic performance led to his being selected to deliver the valedictory speech to his fellow graduating students, he was later awarded his Master of Law and Doctor of Civil Law from the University of Santo Tomas. Perhaps unusually for a lawyer, he was also a body builder and wrestler. He went on to become a leading scholar of civil law. He was a member of the committee that drafted the Civil Code of the Philippines in 1948-49 – which codified the laws governing family and property in the Philippines – and authored the Anti-Graft and Corrupt Practices Act of 1960. He served as Senator from 1957 to 1972 and held the Senate Presidency from 1965 to 1966. In 1986 he served briefly as Vice President of the Philippines, and later served again in the Senate, from 1992-1995.

It was in the arena of international maritime law that Senator Tolentino would make perhaps his most enduring contribution to the nation. As early as the 1958 First Conference on the Law of the Sea, Senator Tolentino – then serving as chairman of the Philippine delegation – had advanced what became known as the "archipelagic principle." This principle held that an archipelago should be regarded as a single geographical, political and economic unit, with the waters between its islands forming part of its internal waters, rather than being treated as "high seas" open to unrestricted foreign navigation.

As Senator Tolentino said during the UNCLOS debate, "An archipelago must be basically considered as an integral geographical entity, strengthened by political and economic unity, and, in some cases, sustained through the years by historical continuity, from which it derives its identity. Thus, an archipelago may have some or all of these factors but the fundamental consideration is that they must have always been identified as one state and one nation. Otherwise, the archipelago may be splintered into as many islands as compose it, with the consequent fragmentation of the nation and the state itself."[84]

The issue was of existential importance for the Philippines, which comprised more than 7,000 islands. If each island were treated separately under traditional maritime law, the Philippines would control only small strips of territorial seas around each different island, with vast stretches of international waters in between, cutting through the archipelago's vital sea arteries. Foreign vessels, including military ships, would have the right to navigate freely through what Filipinos had always rightly considered their own waters. The territorial integrity of the nation would be impossible to maintain.

Tolentino's task was to establish the principle that the Philippine archipelago should be seen as a whole, and not as a collection of islands. The concept faced strong opposition, because the established maritime powers feared that archipelagic nations would claim control over vital maritime straits, creating a potential threat to global freedom of navigation.

The "archipelagic principle" hinged on the concepts of "baselines" – cartographical lines connecting coastal features that would define the starting point of a nation's territorial waters. At its simplest, a coastal baseline is the low-tide mark of a country's coastline. Where the coast is heavily indented with bays and estuaries, or where there are islands just off the coast that belong to the country, it is acceptable to draw a baseline in a straight line from the outermost points of land, including offshore islands. In the case of archipelagic nations, an additional peripheral baseline follows the outer edge of the archipelago as a whole, connecting island to island.

During the UNCLOS III debates, which ran from 1973 to 1982, Senator Tolentino led key sessions of the Philippine delegation, working alongside representatives from other archipelagic states – Indonesia, Fiji, and Mauritius in particular – to build support for the archipelagic doctrine. The conference employed a consensus-based process rather than majority voting, in an attempt to prevent domination by any particular group of nations. With more than 160 nations participating, negotiations were long and difficult. Nations such as Indonesia were reluctant to allow free transit of international shipping through vital navigational channels such as the Malaccan and Sunda Straits.

China, having joined the United Nations in 1971, saw UNCLOS as its first major multilateral negotiation on the world stage. Intriguingly, in the light of its more recent behavior, China sided with developing nations against what it saw as the "hegemonic" powers of the US and USSR.

During the later arbitration between the Philippines and China over China's claims to sovereignty over vast swaths of the South China Sea, one of the Philippine's lawyers, Bernard Oxman, reminded the court of China's stance at the time. "Here's what China said in 1974, at the critical formative session of [UNCLOS]." Oxman told the judges. "'The Asian, African, and Latin American peoples' [said China at that time] 'had long suffered from aggression and plunder at the hands of the colonialists and imperialists and, accordingly, their determination to see a territorial sea established together with an exclusive economic zone up to 200 nautical miles was entirely proper and reasonable.'" China even objected to the UNCLOS ruling that foreign nations should be permitted to fish in other nation's EEZ, if that nation was not able to harvest 100% of the allowable catch. As Oxman told the court, China's position at the time had been that: "To place restrictions on coastal State sovereignty over the resources of the economic zone or on coastal State jurisdiction was to deny the 'exclusive' nature of that zone and was absolutely impermissible."[85] It seems that at the time of the creation of UNCLOS, China had been a staunch and even a "maximalist" supporter of nations' rights to their own EEZ. As one commentator wrote in *The Diplomat* in 2016, "The U.S. and USSR tried hard to limit weaker states' maritime rights by reducing the size of the territorial sea and Exclusive Economic Zone (EEZ). The Chinese delegation saw things from the perspective of a class struggle between the hegemonic and Third World countries."[86]

The irony of this position would become apparent decades later, when China would become one of the most flagrant violators of the very UNCLOS provisions it had championed, using precisely the kind of coercive, might-makes-right approach it had once condemned as “hegemonic”. As James Kraska, Professor of International Maritime Law in the Stockton Center for International Law at the US Naval War College, wrote in an article for *The Diplomat:* “China was a leader among the developing states pushing for increased and secure offshore fishing and mineral rights for coastal states. Now a first order power, China takes it all back. It is as though the United States, Japan and Russia, who successfully bargained for liberal rules to protect freedom of navigation in exchange for recognizing the EEZ, agreed to give up the right to distant water fishing. Then decades after signing the treaty, the maritime powers began again sending industrial factory fishing vessels to scour the EEZs of the developing world.” 87

The breakthrough in the UNCLOS negotiations came when the archipelagic states proposed clear, quantitative limits on how baselines could be drawn. The baselines would have to enclose the main islands of the archipelago with an agreed enclosed water-to-land ratio. The baseline segments could generally not exceed 100 nautical miles (nm), with only a small percentage permitted to reach 125nm, to prevent the drawing of extravagantly long baselines between distant features. Crucially, while archipelagic states would exercise sovereignty over their archipelagic waters, they would allow “innocent passage” of foreign vessels and could be required to designate sea lanes for international navigation – an issue that would form the basis of the Philippine Archipelagic Sea Lanes Act of 2024, which I later helped usher through the Philippine Senate.

In the end, the trade-off at UNCLOS proved to be between the recognition of an EEZ for archipelagic straits and free passage of shipping through the waters of those states. As Kraska wrote in his *Diplomat* article, "[Countries such as Malaysia and Indonesia] relented (…) because the benefits of the package deal, foremost of which included a 200nm EEZ, overcame their hesitancy on free navigation. If you want to get something in maritime diplomacy – exclusive control over an area of ocean – you have to give something in return if the rest of the world is going to cede its rights."[88]

When UNCLOS was finally opened for signature on December 10, 1982, in Montego Bay, Jamaica, the convention codified the archipelagic doctrine. It was a triumph for the Philippines and for Senator Tolentino personally. The archipelagic doctrine is now enshrined in Article I of the Philippine Constitution, which declares that "The national territory comprises the Philippine archipelago, with all the islands and waters embraced therein, and all other territories over which the Philippines has sovereignty or jurisdiction, consisting of its terrestrial, fluvial and aerial domains, including its territorial sea, the seabed, the subsoil, the insular shelves, and other submarine areas. The waters around, between, and connecting the islands of the archipelago, regardless of their breadth and dimensions, form part of the internal waters of the Philippines."[89]

Senator Tolentino's contribution extended beyond the archipelagic doctrine itself. He was instrumental in the broader UNCLOS negotiations, bringing his expertise in international law and his deep understanding of the Philippines' strategic position to bear on questions of maritime zones, resource rights and dispute resolution. His work helped establish the legal framework that would later allow the Philippines to challenge China's expansive claims in the South China Sea through arbitration under the auspices of UNCLOS – the key rulings of which I was later able to help enact into Philippine law.

The Philippines had enacted legislation in 1961 to define its baselines, but these laws were not fully compliant with UNCLOS. It was not until 2009 that Congress passed the Philippine Archipelagic Baselines Law, to bring the country's domestic law into full alignment with its UNCLOS obligations. There were objections – the Philippines' maritime boundaries had previously been defined as those set out in the 1898 Treaty of Paris, in which Spain formally ceded colonial territories such as Cuba, Puerto Rico and the Philippines to the US following the latter's victory in the Spanish-American War. Under that treaty, the Philippines' borders were set as a huge rectangle, encompassing sea hundreds of miles from any coast. These Treaty of Paris boundaries were also built into the Philippine's earlier constitutions. Two legal experts sued the government, arguing that the new baselines were unconstitutional because of this, and that they reduced the Philippines' territory and opened up Philippine waters to foreign shipping.

The case finally came to the Supreme Court, under Justice Antonio Carpio, and was unanimously rejected. The court argued that the new baselines were compliant with UNCLOS, which did not set out national boundaries but merely defined key maritime zones, such as the EEZ. The court also confirmed that the law was not abandoning the Treaty of Paris and that it did not cede any of the Philippine's sovereignty over its internal waters, but allowed it to regulate other nation's right of "innocent passage".

Speaking many years after the famous ruling, Justice Carpio said that the Philippines had "put our house in order by bringing our archipelagic baselines into conformity with UNCLOS so that we could go to an UNCLOS tribunal with clean hands."

Carpio knew that the Philippines would have to be able to demonstrate to the court of arbitration that it was itself compliant with all UNCLOS rulings on baselines, and that they could not validly contest China's "historic" nine-dash line if the Philippines was itself relying on its own "historic line" – the maritime boundaries set by the Treaty of Paris – no matter how valid that historic claim might be. The battle at arbitration would have to be fought on UNCLOS's own rules.[90]

The UNCLOS convention that emerged from nearly a decade of negotiations addressed virtually every aspect of ocean use and governance. It expanded territorial seas from the traditional 3nm to 12nm. It also defined a "contiguous zone" which may extend up to 24nm from the baseline. In this zone, the coastal state doesn't exercise full sovereignty but has powers to prevent people who might be planning an infringement of four specified sets of laws – customs, fiscal, immigration, or sanitary laws – within the state's territory or territorial sea, and to pursue people who have committed offences before they escape into international waters.

The convention created the all-important EEZ, extending 200nm from a nation's baselines, within which coastal states have sovereign rights to explore, exploit, conserve, and manage both living and non-living resources. It established rules for the continental shelf, for international straits, for marine scientific research, for the protection of the marine environment, and for the settlement of disputes via the Permanent Court of Arbitration, the world's oldest court for the settlement of international disputes, established in 1899 as part of the First Hague Peace Conference.

One of the most consequential – and contested – provisions of UNCLOS is an Article titled "Regime of Islands." This Article establishes critical distinctions between the different types of maritime features, with profound implications for the extent of maritime zones they can generate.

An island is defined as "a naturally formed area of land, surrounded by water, which is above water at high tide." The feature must be naturally formed – artificial islands built through land reclamation do not qualify. It must be surrounded by water and must remain above water at high tide. Islands generate the same maritime zones as any other land territory: a territorial sea, a contiguous zone, an EEZ and a continental shelf. Islands are distinguished from 'rocks' – features that cannot sustain human habitation or economic life of their own. Even more fundamental is the distinction between high-tide features and low-tide elevations. Article 13 of UNCLOS defines a low-tide elevation as "a naturally formed area of land which is surrounded by and above water at low tide but submerged at high tide." Low-tide elevations generate no maritime zones of their own. If a low-tide elevation is located within the territorial sea of an island or the mainland, it may be used as a baseline point from which to measure the breadth of the territorial sea. But if it lies beyond the territorial sea, it has no legal significance for maritime zones whatsoever.

The convention also addressed the issue that had inspired Arvid Pardo's original 1967 speech: the resources of the deep seabed beyond national jurisdiction. Part XI of UNCLOS established the International Seabed Authority to manage these resources as the "common heritage of mankind." This proved to be the most contentious part of the convention. The United States and several other industrialized nations objected to provisions they saw as hostile to private enterprise and free-market principles. It was not until 1994, when an implementing agreement substantially modified Part XI to remove the more “redistributive” elements of Pardo's original vision and establish a free-market framework, that the convention could enter into force.

Pardo was bitterly disappointed at the compromises that had been made at the expense of his vision of a “common heritage” that would be used to raise the poorer nations of the earth, saying that "All that is left of the common heritage of mankind is a few fish and a little seaweed." The Secretary General of the UN at time of the convention's signing in 1982, Javier Pérez de Cuéllar, was more optimistic, and more accurate, saying that UNCLOS was "possibly the most significant legal instrument of this century."[91]

On November 16, 1994, one year after Guyana became the sixtieth nation to ratify the treaty – the necessary threshold for the treaty to take force – UNCLOS became international law. Today, 169 sovereign states and the European Union are parties to the convention. The United States, despite having participated actively in the negotiations and despite recognizing UNCLOS as a codification of customary international law, has still not ratified it – a fact that diminishes America's ability to shape the interpretation and application of its provisions.

For the Philippines, UNCLOS represented the culmination of decades of advocacy. The convention that came into force in 1994 was built, in part, on the foundation laid by lolo "Turing" Tolentino and other Filipino diplomats who had fought to ensure that the law of the sea would reflect not just the interests of the great naval powers, but the legitimate rights and needs of archipelagic states, coastal developing nations, and all countries that depend on the oceans for their security and prosperity.

The principles established in UNCLOS – the breadth of territorial waters, the rights associated with the EEZ, the limitations on what features can generate maritime zones and the procedures for dispute resolution – would become central to the Philippines' ongoing struggle to defend its maritime territory in the West Philippine Sea. Without UNCLOS, China's expansive claims based on vague "historic rights" would have been far more difficult to challenge. With UNCLOS, the Philippines would have a legal framework recognized by the international community, and a mechanism – arbitration – to seek a binding ruling on the validity of those claims.

CHAPTER 6

The Road to the Hague

Fretti Ganchoon is currently Senior State Counsel at the Philippines' Department of Justice (DOJ). She is the head of Legal Staff for Maritime Affairs and representative to the National Task Force for the West Philippine Sea (NTF-WPS) and the National Maritime Council (NMC).

When she joined the DOJ as State Counsel in 2007, Ganchoon was assigned to attend meetings at the Commission on Maritime and Occean Affairs. It could never have occurred to her at the time that this simple assignment would soon place her at the heart of one of the most significant legal proceedings in the Philippines' history.

I talked to Ganchoon about those early days at the DOJ.

"I joined the DOJ in 2007," she told me, "And they just decided, 'She's new, perhaps we'll give her this maritime portfolio.' I did not exclusively handle it at first – two senior lawyers would attend the meetings with me. But after two years, those two senior lawyers got involved with trade and other matters, and so I was the one who was left handling the maritime portfolios. I would say that starting 2008 or 2009, I became the focal attorney or lawyer or

State Counsel at the Department of Justice for maritime matters."

In 2012, following the momentous decisions to take China to the PCA, Ganchoon found herself deeply involved in the preparations for the case.

"The decision to file a case, of course, was made by the President himself. The one who approached the Department of Justice was the Office of the Solicitor General, which is an agency attached to the Department of Justice, and usually they are the ones who would handle international cases. Our office also has an international aspect to our work, but when it comes to organizing a team for the filing of an international case, usually it would be the Office of the Solicitor General. The Solicitor General at the time was Francis Jardeleza.

"Before the Office of the Solicitor General approached the Department of Justice to be a part of this team, there had already been some preparatory work at the Department of Foreign Affairs. So there's the Department of Foreign affairs, the Solicitor General, and then the Department of Justice. I was a junior lawyer still at that time, but since it was a maritime matter, it was referred to me. I assisted the head of our office, the Chief State Counsel, and both of us assisted the Secretary of Justice. All of those preparations took place in 2012, and it was only three of us – Laila de Lima, the Secretary of Justice, Ricardo Parras, the Chief State Council, and me, State Counsel Fretti Ganchoon."

Ganchoon told me about the great secrecy behind the case.

"In my view at that time, the strategy really came from the Department of Foreign affairs in coordination with retired Supreme Court Senior Associate Justice Carpio, who were talking to one another. Then of course there were lawyers from the DOJ and from the Office of the Solicitor General studying their proposals to ensure they were legally sound. A key question was who would be the Foreign Counsel that would be appointed to represent the Philippines, which is why they went to Washington D.C. in August and September of that year in order to talk to law firms and determine which would be recommended to be hired as the Foreign Counsel of the Republic of the Philippines. Everything was under wraps. It was super secret at the time so that nobody would know that the Philippines was actually quite serious in filing a case against China."

Foreign Affairs Secretary Albert del Rosario and Solicitor General Francis Jardeleza assigned two Department of Foreign Affairs (DFA) lawyers to look for law firms who were best able to represent the Philippines in their arbitration.

One lawyer was assigned to Europe. They interviewed lawyers from five different law firms specializing in the law of the sea. According to Marites Vitug, writing in *Rock Solid,* "[the DFA lawyer] recalled that of the five, three could not accept the case because China was their client. One lawyer said he would consult his principal (a state) and declined because his principal had good relations with China. The fifth did not qualify. Early on, the influence of China was already palpable, spreading even to law firms."[92]

Luckily, the team in Washington D.C. fared better. They were particularly impressed by Paul Reichler of the law firm Foley Hoag. Reichler had represented several high-profile international cases, including one in which Nicaragua was awarded additional maritime territory by the International Court of Justice following a dispute with its larger neighbor, Colombia. In another major case, Reichler had represented the island of Mauritius, a former British Colony, in its dispute over Great Britain's sovereignty over the Chagos Islands, which it had separated from Mauritius before it gained independence in 1968. Reichler greatly impressed the DFA lawyer, and Foley Hoag were eventually appointed.

The decision to take China to the PCA was announced by Rosario on January 22, 2013. In his statement, Rosario said, "This afternoon, the Philippines has taken the step of bringing China before an Arbitral Tribunal under Article 287 and Annex VII of the 1982 United Nations Convention on the Law of the Sea (UNCLOS) in order to achieve a peaceful and durable solution to the dispute over the West Philippine Sea (WPS)."[93]

Rosario's statement said that the Chinese Ambassador had been summoned to the DFA at around one o'clock that afternoon and handed a note verbale challenging the validity of "China's nine-dash line claim to almost the entire South China Sea" and asking China to "desist from unlawful activities that violate the sovereign rights and jurisdiction of the Philippines under the 1982 UNCLOS."

The statement continued: "The Philippines has exhausted almost all political and diplomatic avenues for a peaceful negotiated settlement of its maritime dispute with China. (…) To this day, a solution is still elusive. We hope that the Arbitral Proceedings shall bring this dispute to a durable solution."

The Chinese Ambassador rejected the note verbale and a Chinese spokesperson told the press that "The note and related notice not only violate the consensus enshrined in the Declaration on the Conduct of Parties in the South China Sea (DOC), but are also factually flawed and contain false accusations." The spokesperson reiterated China's usual request for "dialogue": "China hopes the Philippines will honor its commitment by not taking any action that could complicate the issue, positively respond to China's proposal to establish a bilateral dialogue mechanism on maritime issues and work to solve the issue through bilateral negotiations." [94] It was the usual approach of China of calling for "bilateral negotiations" while refusing to address the core issue of China's unjustified claims of sovereignty.

Much as China may have wanted to avoid arbitration, it had no choice in the matter.

Part XV of UNCLOS covers the procedures that would deal with disputes between nations about the interpretation or application of the Convention. Under Article 286, disputes that cannot be settled by negotiation or other peaceful means may be submitted to a court or tribunal having jurisdiction. Article 287 gives states a choice of dispute settlement procedures, including the International Tribunal for the Law of the Sea, the International Court of Justice, an arbitral tribunal constituted under Annex VII, or a special arbitral tribunal constituted under Annex VIII. If disputing parties fail on agree on the same procedure, the dispute may only be submitted to arbitration under Annex VII at the Permanent Court of Arbitration (PCA) in The Hague, the Netherlands.

Article 296 provides that any decision rendered by a court or tribunal having jurisdiction under Part XV "shall be final and shall be complied with by all the parties to the dispute." If China refused to take part in the arbitration process – which was highly likely – that would not change this legal fact. Article 11 of Annex VII makes clear that the absence of a party to the dispute "shall not constitute a bar to the proceedings," and the court's ruling would be final and binding on both parties.

Despite having refused to participate in the arbitration proceedings, China released a 93-paragraph Position Paper in December 2014 – nearly two years after the Philippines filed its case – arguing that the tribunal lacked jurisdiction. The paper repeated the usual sweeping sovereignty claims: "China has indisputable sovereignty over the South China Sea Islands (…) and the adjacent waters," stating, without evidence, that "Chinese activities in the South China Sea date back to over 2,000 years ago" and that "China was the first country to discover, name, explore and exploit the resources of the South China Sea Islands and the first to continuously exercise sovereign powers over them." The paper also accused the Philippines of having "illegally occupied a number of maritime features of China's *Nansha* [Spratly] Islands" and of having "violated the Charter of the United Nations and international law, and seriously encroached upon China's territorial sovereignty."[95]

The primary argument of the Position Paper was that the dispute between the Philippines and China was fundamentally about territorial sovereignty, which falls outside UNCLOS jurisdiction. But the Philippines were well aware of this, and had asked the PCA to rule, not on the question of ownership of various features but on the maritime entitlements of various types of feature and on whether China's claims to sovereignty inside the nine-dash line had any legal basis under UNCLOS that would allow China to claim resources within the Philippines' EEZ – something that was entirely and precisely within the PCA's remit.

China was clearly aware of the danger the arbitration process posed for their unsubstantiated claims of sovereignty. The Position Paper complained that "the Philippines has cunningly packaged its case in the present form." The paper also complained that the Philippines was being "increasingly provocative" and painted China as the victim, saying it had been "forced to take necessary measures in response to (...) provocative conduct." The document concluded by declaring that the arbitration "will not change the history and fact of China's sovereignty" and "will not shake China's resolve and determination." The entire paper adopted an intriguingly inconsistent approach, simultaneously claiming the tribunal had no authority while arguing China's case passionately – the legal equivalent of boycotting a trial while submitting a defense.

CHAPTER 7

The Arbitral Ruling

On July 12, 2016, in The Hague, at precisely 11:00 a.m., the Permanent Court of Arbitration (PCA) released its ruling in the case of *The Republic of the Philippines v. The People's Republic of China*. The award ran to 479 pages of dense legal analysis, examining thousands of pages of evidence, historical records, expert testimony, and maritime surveys. But its core findings could be summarized in a handful of devastating conclusions that would reshape the legal landscape of the South China Sea: China's expansive claims had no basis in international law.

For the Philippines, it was an overwhelming legal victory. For China, it was a ruling they had spent three and a half years insisting would be "null and void."

Within hours of the ruling's release, China's Foreign Ministry issued a statement declaring exactly that: the award was "null and void" and that "The Chinese government and the Chinese people firmly oppose [the ruling] and will neither acknowledge it nor accept it."[96] But the legal earthquake had already taken place. The tribunal had systematically dismantled the foundation of China's South China Sea claims, brick by legal brick. The empty chair at the arbitration proceedings – China's deliberate absence throughout – had not prevented justice from being done.

The tribunal's most consequential finding addressed the issue at the heart of everything: China's nine-dash line.

For decades, China had maintained that it possessed “historic rights” to the resources within the nine-dash line - that vague, coordinates-free boundary encompassing nearly the entire South China Sea that had first begun to appear on maps, without explanation, in 1936. These "historic rights," China claimed, predated UNCLOS and therefore superseded it. It was a claim that, if accepted, would have rendered meaningless the Economic Exclusion Zone (EEZ) rights that UNCLOS granted to all coastal states, such as the Philippines. China's position, in essence, was that the Philippines might have an EEZ under UNCLOS, but China's “historic rights” took precedence within the nine-dash line, allowing China to fish, explore for oil and gas, and exercise jurisdiction over an ocean area almost the size of the Mediterranean Sea which also included large parts of several other nations’ legally-established EEZs.

The tribunal rejected this argument entirely.

The tribunal had examined Chinese historical records, imperial maps, and documented activities in the South China Sea over centuries. What they found was telling: there was no evidence that China had historically exercised exclusive control over the waters of the South China Sea or prevented other nations from exploiting their resources. Chinese fishermen had visited the area. Chinese dynasties had sent naval expeditions through these waters. But visiting and controlling are very different things under international law. Historic use by Chinese fishermen did not translate into Chinese sovereignty over the waters themselves, any more than did the fishing activities – over many millennia – of the other nations in the area.

UNCLOS had fundamentally changed the legal landscape. Article 311 of UNCLOS makes clear that the Convention supersedes earlier agreements and claims that are inconsistent with it. When China ratified UNCLOS in 1996, it accepted a comprehensive regime for maritime entitlements that replaced any pre-existing claims based on historic use. UNCLOS created a new legal order for the oceans – one based on clear rules about baselines, territorial seas and EEZs, not on vague assertions about ancient fishing grounds or imperial tribute systems.

As the tribunal noted, "Although Chinese navigators and fishermen, as well as those of other States, had historically made use of the islands in the South China Sea, there was no evidence that China had historically exercised exclusive control over the waters or their resources. The Tribunal concluded that there was no legal basis for China to claim historic rights to resources within the sea areas falling within the 'nine-dash line.'"

This single finding invalidated the foundation of China's entire position. Everything China had done in the South China Sea – the artificial islands built on virgin reefs, the military installations, the harassment of Philippine vessels, the prevention of oil and gas exploration at Recto Bank – rested on claims that an international tribunal had now determined had no basis in law. The nine-dash line, legally speaking, was meaningless – something that had been obvious to every nation other than China from the moment the line made in first shaky appearance on Chinese maps.

The tribunal's second major set of findings concerned the status of individual maritime features in the South China Sea. This was where the technical precision of UNCLOS Article 121 became crucial – and where the tribunal's findings would prove devastating to China's territorial ambitions.

Under UNCLOS, the classification of a feature determines what maritime zones it can generate. An island, defined as "a naturally formed area of land, surrounded by water, which is above water at high tide", generates a 12 nautical mile (nm) territorial sea, a 24nm contiguous zone, a 200nm EEZ and continental shelf rights.

However, not every piece of land that is surrounded by sea is an island: some – as we saw earlier – are merely rocks, defined as features "which cannot sustain human habitation or economic life of their own". Rocks have no EEZ or continental shelf and are entitled only to a 12-nautical-mile territorial sea, nothing more.

Features that are submerged at high tide – low-tide elevations – generate no maritime zones. They have no maritime entitlements unless they fall within the territorial sea of a legitimate island or mainland coast, in which case they come under the sovereignty of the coastal state and can be used in the drawing up of baselines to extend the territorial sea.

The tribunal examined each of the significant features in the Spratly Islands that China claimed or had occupied. The Philippines' legal team had submitted detailed evidence: historical accounts from British naval surveys, the logs of nineteenth-century mariners, Japanese military records from World War II, current scientific assessments of each feature's capacity to support human life. The tribunal reviewed all these materials with great care.

Their findings were devastating to China's position.

Panatag (Scarborough) Shoal, the site of the 2012 standoff that had triggered the arbitration, was a rock. It could generate a 12nm territorial sea, but no EEZ. The tribunal found that the feature "has no fresh water, no natural vegetation, and very limited soil," that it "cannot be inhabited in its natural condition," and that "there is no contemporaneous evidence that it has historically sustained human habitation." Even though China had forcibly occupied Panatag Shoal and driven Filipino fishermen from their traditional fisheries, this occupation gave China no rights to an EEZ – and seizing territory by force had been illegal since the post-WWII UN Charter of 1945.

Panganiban (Mischief) Reef, where China had built its first structure in the Spratlys back in 1995, claiming to be constructing "fishermen's shelters," was not even a rock. It was a low-tide elevation, submerged at high tide. Under UNCLOS, it generated no maritime zones at all. The tribunal found it was located on the Philippines' continental shelf and within the Philippine EEZ. China's occupation had been unlawful from the beginning.

Mabini (Johnson South) Reef, Calderon (Cuarteron) Reef, and Kagitingan (Fiery Cross) Reef – the features China had seized in 1988 in the violent confrontations with Vietnam – were all rocks, incapable of generating an EEZ.

Burgos (Gaven) Reef was also a rock, and Zamora (Subi) Reef and McKennan (Hughes) Reef – all also occupied in 1988 – were low-tide elevations, just like Panganiban Reef.

The tribunal went further still. It examined Itu Aba (*Taiping*) Island, the largest naturally formed feature in the Spratly Islands, controlled by Taiwan. Taiwan had built an airstrip there, constructed buildings, drilled a well for fresh water. Surely if any feature in the Spratlys could qualify as an island capable of generating an EEZ, it would be Itu Aba.

The tribunal disagreed. Even Itu Aba, the tribunal found, was a rock.

Despite being over 1.4 kilometers long and 400 meters wide and arguably having "fresh" (though barely potable) water, the Tribunal judged that Itu Aba could not "sustain human habitation or economic life of its own" as required by Article 121(3). Though there had been fresh water on the island, overextraction had made what water remained too salty to drink and Taiwanese troops had been forced to construct desalination plants to supply fresh water. There was no topsoil, and no agriculture. Taiwanese troops grew a few plants for the pleasure of gardening and to supplement their supplies, but even the soil they used was delivered from the mainland. Permanent habitation required continuous outside support – regular supply ships bringing food, fuel, medicine, and building materials. Itu Abba was not a feature that could sustain human habitation "of its own."

The implications were staggering: none of the naturally formed features in the Spratly Islands – not one – qualified as an island capable of generating an EEZ. China's massive island-building program, its seizing of reefs and their transformation into military fortresses with runways and hangars and missile shelters, had generated no new maritime entitlements whatsoever. You cannot change a rock or a low-tide elevation into an island that generates an EEZ by piling dredged sand on top of it and pouring on concrete. The legal status of a feature, under UNCLOS, is determined by its natural condition, not by what humans build on it. And since China's nine-dash line had been ruled to have no legal status, and seizing territory by force had been illegal since the 1945 UN Charter, China's presence on these features was itself illegal.

Because none of China's claimed features could generate an EEZ, the tribunal could make determinations about maritime entitlements in certain areas without needing to delimit any boundary between the Philippines and China.

The tribunal found that Panganiban, Ayungin and Recto Bank all fell within the Philippine EEZ and were on the Philippine continental shelf. These areas, the tribunal declared, were "not overlapped by any possible entitlement of China" – a hugely significant ruling.

The Philippines' sovereign rights in these areas were clear and uncontestable under UNCLOS. China's presence at Mischief Reef – its construction of a massive artificial island complete with runways, hangars, and missile shelters – was a violation of Philippine sovereign rights. China's 2011 harassment of the survey vessel at Recto Bank – the incident that had prevented the Philippines from exploring its own oil and gas resources – was unlawful. China's repeated attempts to prevent the Philippines from resupplying the tiny garrison aboard the BRP *Sierra Madre* – which had been deliberately grounded *o*n Ayungin Shoal (Second Thomas Shoal) in 1999 and permanently occupied by Philippine troops ever since as proof of Philippine sovereignty – were violations of international law.

The tribunal also found that China had violated its obligations under UNCLOS in numerous other ways.

Chinese law enforcement vessels had unlawfully created a serious risk of collision with Philippine vessels through their dangerous maneuvers. China had unlawfully prevented Philippine fishermen from pursuing their traditional livelihood at Panatag (Scarborough) Shoal. After the 2012 standoff, when Chinese vessels blockaded the shoal, preventing Filipino fishermen from entering while allowing Chinese fishermen free access, this violated traditional fishing rights that UNCLOS recognizes and protects.

China had unlawfully failed to prevent Chinese fishermen from fishing in the Philippine EEZ. Under UNCLOS, a coastal state has sovereign rights to manage the resources in its EEZ. China's failure to stop its fishermen from operating in Philippine waters without permission was a violation of the Philippines' rights.

The tribunal also found that China had caused "severe harm to the coral reef environment" at seven features in the Spratly Islands through its land reclamation activities and construction of artificial islands.

The environmental findings were truly shocking. The tribunal reviewed evidence of how Chinese dredging had destroyed vast areas of coral reef – fragile ecosystems that had taken millennia to develop. Entire reef structures had been destroyed by the dredging process or subsequently buried under millions of tons of sand and coral debris. The tribunal noted that "China's dredging and construction activities have caused devastating and long-lasting damage to the marine environment."

Chinese fishermen were also found to have harvested giant clams on a huge scale. These enormous mollusks, some weighing hundreds of kilograms, take decades to grow to maturity. They were being torn from the seabed or the reefs themselves and killed. Their meat was sold as a delicacy. The giant shells were sold as decorative items or ground up and used in traditional medicines. The Philippines presented evidence to the tribunal showing that "the harvesting of giant clams in the South China Sea has been so intense in recent years that the population of these species has been almost completely depleted."

The tribunal found that China had violated its obligation under UNCLOS Article 192 to "protect and preserve the marine environment." This was not mere academic criticism. The environmental destruction China had caused was, as the tribunal noted, "irreversible."

The award was everything the Philippines had hoped for – and more.

It validated the decision to pursue arbitration, vindicated Justice Antonio Carpio's vision of law as the great equalizer between small nations and superpowers and honored the legal framework that Senator Arturo Tolentino had helped create decades earlier in the form of UNCLOS. The principles he had fought for – the archipelagic doctrine, the EEZ, the regime of islands, with its crucial distinction between islands and rocks – had been applied by an international tribunal to protect the Philippines from a far more powerful neighbor.

The legal architecture that the great mind of Senator Arturo Tolentino had helped build had worked exactly as it was supposed to. The nine-dash line and China's "historic rights" claim had no legal basis. The features China had militarized could not generate the maritime zones China claimed. The waters China sought to control belonged, under law, to the Philippines.

China's immediate and total rejection of the ruling did nothing to diminish its legal force. Under UNCLOS Article 296, awards are "final and shall be complied with by all the parties to the dispute." This was not a recommendation or an advisory opinion, it was a legally binding judgment.

But legal obligations and practical enforcement are different matters. The Philippines had won a resounding legal victory, but the tribunal had no mechanism to compel China's compliance. There was no international police force to prevent Chinese vessels from harassing Philippine fishermen or to force China to dismantle its artificial islands and remove their garrisons. The award carried the full weight of international law, but all law is dependent on the will of those bound by that law to behave lawfully. China, as one of the five permanent members of the UN Security Council, could veto any attempt to enforce the ruling through that body. The United States, though it was supportive of the ruling and had conducted "freedom of navigation operations" near China's artificial islands with US naval vessels to demonstrate that these features generated no lawful territorial seas, had not itself ratified UNCLOS. Chinese officials were quick to point out that America was demanding Chinese compliance with a treaty the US itself had refused to ratify.

Nevertheless, the award had established, with the authority of international law, the truth about the South China Sea. The facts were now a matter of record, examined and verified by independent judges.

The Aquino administration, which had initiated the case and seen it through to victory, set out to rally regional and global support for the ruling and to make China's non-compliance as costly as possible in diplomatic terms. But in 2016, the Philippines were in the middle of a presidential transition. Rodrigo Duterte was elected as the new President, and his approach to China would prove radically different from his predecessor's. He saw opportunities for Chinese investment and infrastructure funding and argued that quiet diplomacy and personal relationships could secure better outcomes than confrontation. Duterte spoke of the arbitral ruling as "just a piece of paper" that he would "throw away."[97]

In 2018, as we saw earlier, his administration signed a Memorandum of Understanding with China on joint oil and gas exploration – though that agreement would ultimately come to nothing when China refused to accept any framework that confirmed Philippine sovereignty over the resources. The massive inward investment from China that Duterte had hoped for similarly failed to materialize. In a 2016 visit to China, Duterte had been promised $24 billion in investment in major infrastructure projects. Few came to fruition.

For a time, the arbitral award became something of a "legal orphan" – a potentially powerful instrument with no one willing or able to give it legal force. Nevertheless, the ruling was not forgotten. Persuasive advocates such as Justice Carpio continued to speak and write about it, keeping it in the public eye. International lawyers cited the award as a landmark case in maritime law. Regional neighbors – and the wider world – watched China's continued island-building and their militarization of the South China Sea with alarm. Within the Philippine government and civil service, politicians and lawyers who understood the ruling's importance waited for a political moment when it could be revived – as I did myself.

The 2022 election of President Ferdinand Marcos Jr. created a new environment. Marcos set out to defend Philippine maritime rights, strengthening ties with traditional allies such as the United States and challenging China's aggressive stance.

This is where my own part in the story truly begins.

As a Senator of the Philippines, I would become the principal author of the Philippine Maritime Zones Act – legislation that would enshrine the core principles of the 2016 arbitral award into Philippine domestic law. The Act would define and assert the Philippines' rights to all its maritime zones in accordance with UNCLOS and the tribunal's findings. It would explicitly reject China's nine-dash line in Philippine law and assert Philippine sovereignty over waters the tribunal had confirmed belonged to the Philippines.

I would also be the principal author of the Philippine Archipelagic Sea Lanes Act – legislation that would implement another crucial UNCLOS provision by designating sea lanes through Philippine archipelagic waters where foreign vessels could exercise the right of innocent passage, while asserting Philippine sovereignty over the waters themselves.

Both pieces of legislation would pass unanimously through the Philippine Senate and House of Representatives, though not before I had spent many arduous months working to get the bill passed, and anxious weeks waiting for the Executive to finally sign the Acts into law, as I will recount in a later chapter. Both would be signed into law by President Marcos – and both would trigger immediate condemnation from China, culminating in my being personally banned from entering Chinese territory, a prohibition I wear as a badge of honor, as I said in the Introduction to this book.

The battle to implement the arbitral award through domestic legislation, the diplomatic confrontations that ensued and China's furious response are the subject of the next chapters. But they all trace back to the PCA award of July 12, 2016, and to those hundreds of pages of legal reasoning that declared, definitively and finally, that might does not make right – that the rule of law still matters in international affairs, and that even a superpower must be held accountable when it violates the rights of its smaller neighbors.

The arbitral award had given the Philippines a powerful weapon: the weapon of law. Using that weapon effectively, translating legal victory into practical policy, would prove to be the next great challenge. It was a challenge I was determined to meet.

CHAPTER 8

From Tagaytay to the Senate

It's probably time for me to tell you more about my career. I have deliberately chosen not to make this book about me: the book is about the Philippines and about the future. But it may be useful for you to know something about my journey and how being elected to the Senate eventually gave me the opportunity to help with the passage of two Acts about the Philippines' maritime rights and obligations that I believe are core to our nation's independence.

My family has a long history of public service. We have already seen how my kindred, Senator Arturo Tolentino, played a significant role in the creation of UNCLOS, the vital legal framework that underpins the Acts I have been honored to help pass into Philippine law. I can still remember how Lola Constancia, wife of Senator Arturo Tolentino, would often stay at our family house in Tagaytay.

My father, Isaac Tolentino, was the longest-serving mayor of Tagaytay City, holding office from 1954 to 1980 – twenty-six years dedicated to transforming a city that had been granted its charter as recently as 1938 into one of the Philippines' leading cities. Tagaytay Ridge – about 600 meters above sea level – used to be a hideout for Filipino insurgents during the Philippine Revolution of 1896. Its cool climate and the fact that it was only an hour's drive from Manila made Tagaytay a popular summer retreat in the 1930s for Americans and wealthier Filipinos. By the 1990s, Tagaytay had become a major tourist destination in the region.

While I was growing up in the city, there was a particularly bad typhoon, and our house became the evacuation center for the whole surrounding area. We shared our meals and our blankets with the evacuees. When someone needed to go to hospital, my father would drive them in his car. He would get woken at three in the morning if someone was sick or was giving birth and he would take them to the hospital: my father's car became everyone's ambulance. I grew up with the idea that it was important to try to do something for the community you lived in, and to try to help make people's lives better.

My father's position also meant that I got to know many of the politicians of the day. I met all of the governors of Cavite Province, and I met all the Philippine Presidents of those times: "Old Marcos" (Ferdinand Marcos), Cory (Corazon) Aquino and FVR (Fidel V. Ramos). I won't say that I always dreamed of being a politician, but I did grow up thinking that public service was important and that being a public figure was not something unachievable: I met public figures regularly in our day-to-day life, and they were like family friends – people you could relate to. In the course of my life, I also met – modesty aside – Presidents Obama and Trump, His Holiness the Pope, and other eminent figures.

The law was also always something of interest to me. My father was a lawyer by training and had a big library of books, most of them about the law. My mother used to make my brother and I have a short sleep at noon, but I never wanted to go to sleep, so I used to read my father's books. Even when I didn't understand them, I tried to read them and see if I could learn something. I have a big library at home myself today. In my office at the Senate, I have one of the biggest collections of books of any Senator – or so I believe – most of them about the law.

A career in law was always of interest to me, but when I was young, I also wanted to be a military officer. There is a military high school in Quezon City – the Far East Military Academy – and I was accepted to study there.

Later, I studied at the Citadel, the Military College of South Carolina, and graduated from the Command and General Staff College. But my most significant military education came from the National Defense College of the Philippines (NDCP), where I earned my Masters in National Security Administration, ranking sixth out of 55 graduates – a cohort that included many future senior military officers in all branches of the Armed Forces of the Philippines (AFP).

The NDCP program was transformative. While my classmates were primarily career military officers – men and women who would devote their lives to defending the nation – I was one of the few civilians in the program. We studied everything from strategic thinking to crisis management, from regional security to military operations. The program also included field exercises that took us to the places that would later become flashpoints in the Philippines' struggle to defend its maritime territories. In 1998, I made my first visit to Pag-asa Island in the Kalayaan Island Group. We flew in on a Philippine Air

Force C-130 cargo plane, landing on the island's small airstrip, which was barely long enough to allow the plane to take off again after our visit. We took supplies to the few Filipino soldiers stationed there: food; VHS videotapes for recreation; other necessities. I was struck by the harsh conditions the soldiers put up with on a daily basis, trying to maintain a semblance of normal life while defending Philippine sovereignty in one of the most remote and vulnerable outposts imaginable. Even then, one could see Chinese vessels in the near distance; a hostile presence.

Over time, I rose through the ranks of the Philippine Army Reserve, eventually achieving the rank of Brigadier General. In 2001, I was named AFP Reserve Officer of the Year. My military identity isn't ceremonial; it's a core part of who I am and how I understand the security challenges facing the Philippines.

My military education took place in tandem with my legal education. I gained my Bachelor of Arts in Philosophy and Bachelor of Laws degree from the Ateneo de Manila University and went on to study for my Bachelor of Laws (LLB) at the university's Law School. I eventually gained three Masters of Laws degrees: one from the University of Michigan Law School, where I studied Constitutional Law; one from the University of London, where in studied Public International Law, a specialization that was directly relevant to the maritime disputes that would define my later career; and a third Master's degree from Columbia Law School, where I was awarded an LLM in Corporation Law.

I passed the New York State Bar Examinations in 1991, and for a time I practiced law in New York. I could have forged a lucrative career there, but the pull of home was too strong. The Philippines needed people who understood both international legal frameworks and the unique challenges facing our nation. I felt I had something to offer.

My first taste of public service and of politics had come earlier. In 1986, at the age of only 26, newly installed President Corazon Aquino appointed me Officer-in-Charge (OIC) Mayor of Tagaytay City, filling the role my father had previously held for so long (my father stepped down as mayor in 1980, and died in 2016, at the age of 93.) It was a provisional appointment in the aftermath of the "People Power Revolution'", which is also known to Filipinos as the "EDSA Revolution," but it was my introduction to executive leadership. As all residents of Manila and anyone who has visited the city knows, EDSA stands for Epifanio de los Santos Avenue, a major thoroughfare that serves as a "beltway" encircling Manila; people gathered peacefully on the Avenue to protest against the presidency of Ferdinand Marcos Sr, leading to the election of President Aquino – hence "the EDSA Revolution."

I remember my early days in office very well. I used to go home for lunch every day because there were only three restaurants in Tagaytay at the time; now there are over 300! I served as OIC Mayor for one year, until 1987, and then returned to my studies and to the law. I was elected Mayor of Tagaytay again in 1995, and served for three consecutive terms, until 2004.

There are several projects I initiated during my time as mayor that I still see as important achievements – things that have helped make lives better for the people of Tagaytay. I helped create two centers of education – City College of Tagaytay, and City Science National High School – and Tagaytay Hospital. I established the Tagaytay Public Safety Office, to help manage traffic in the city. I also initiated the "Character First" programs, encouraging local government units, NGOs, civic organizations, and religious groups to work together to establish a "city of character," promoting Filipino values. Later in my political career, I encouraged and supported many small local festivals to help celebrate Filipino culture and our distinctive national character.

In 2010, President Benigno Aquino III appointed me to a role that would put me in the national spotlight: Chairman of the Metropolitan Manila Development Authority (MMDA). I was the first non-resident of Metro Manila to hold this position. There was some grumbling at the time that I was not a "native" of Manila – but you didn't have to be born in Manila to understand the problems the vibrant but overcrowded city, with its struggling infrastructure, was facing.

What I enjoyed most about my time leading the MMDA was the scope to go beyond the routine aspects of the job and set some truly innovative projects in motion – things, again, that would improve people's lives. I implemented many projects to improve the heavily congested EDSA – Epifanio de los Santos Avenue. I introduced dedicated bicycle and motorcycle lanes and enforced the "Yellow Lane" policy for buses. I launched Manila's first Integrated Bus Terminal, preventing regional buses from traveling all the way to the city's center, adding to congestion, and requiring passengers to transfer to local city transport. I banned heavy trucks completely from EDSA and created "vertical gardens" – green walls in road tunnels and hanging baskets on lampposts that absorbed pollution and pleased the eye. I also limited the maximum size of advertising billboards, which helped improve sightlines and safety for motorists but also enhanced the aesthetics of the city. All of this made EDSA a far safer and more pleasant environment for users.

I revived the Pasig River Ferry Service, which had stopped running in 2011, to create an alternative way of getting around the city, getting commuters off the roads and onto the river. In the early days of the ferry, we offered free rides and even free coffee to encourage people to use the service. By the end of 2015, we had 11 operational ferries, including new fiberglass vessels capable of carrying up to 45 passengers each. At one point, we quickly created new ferries by bolting mini-bus bodies onto repurposed tugboats – an excellent example of Filipino innovation and ingenuity. I also started providing real-time traffic updates via social media. It was a time of great innovation and energy, all aimed at making Manila a safer, more efficient and more attractive urban environment. I was also an advocate for disaster preparedness, popularizing the "duck, cover, and hold" routine to help people survive the immediate effects of earthquakes – this so-called "Shake Drill" was the first public earthquake drill to be introduced in the Philippines. When Typhoon Haiyan, known locally as Super Typhoon Yolanda, devastated Tacloban and other parts of Eastern Visayas in November 2013, we were among the first to respond, mobilizing thousands of MMDA personnel and supplying heavy equipment for search and rescue operations.

As MMDA chairman, I was also designated chairman of the annual Metro Manila Film Festival. I introduced reforms, including the introduction of new categories and the removal of box office receipts from the criteria for selecting Best Picture, in an effort to reward artistic merit over commercial considerations – the latest Hollywood blockbusters will always attract audiences; that doesn't necessarily make them the most deserving of awards. I also chaired the centennial anniversary of the Iglesia ni Cristo, an independent Christian church founded in the Philippines in the early 20th century which now has around three million members, which was a great honor for me.

In October 2015, I left the MMDA to pursue a Senate bid in the 2016 National elections, where I placed 13th – just one slot outside the winning circle of 12. From 2017 to 2018, I served as Presidential Adviser on Political Affairs under President Rodrigo Duterte. It was a non-Cabinet portfolio role, but it gave me direct experience of national politics. In 2019, I ran for Senate again and secured 9th place, with 15.5 million votes. I was finally a senator.

I took my seat in the Senate on June 30, 2019. I was named chair of the Senate Committee on Local Government and the Senate Committee on Urban Planning, Housing, and Resettlement, in recognition of my experience as a longtime mayor and MMDA chairman. But from my earliest days as senator, I was vocal about issues that transcended local governance, and especially about Philippine sovereignty in the West Philippine Sea.

As early as 2013, while I was still MMDA chairman, I had given a speech as the guest of honor at an Independence Day celebration at Barsoain Church in Malolos, Bulacan, in Central Luzon. Malolos and the beautiful Barsoain Church have a special place in the hearts of all Filipinos as the site where the first 1899 Philippine Republic's constitution was drawn up by the Philippine Constitutional Convention following the uprising against the Spanish Empire. In that speech, I traced the legal history of Philippine territory through the various treaties that had defined our geography, including the 1900 Treaty of Washington, which clarified the scope of the territories ceded by Spain to the US in the Treaty of Paris, after the Spanish Empire's defeat in the Spanish-American War. I also spoke about Chinese aggression in the West Philippine Sea.

Let us recall the events of recent months, when we received distressing reports that a powerful nation continues to occupy and claim our small islands in the West Philippine Sea, including Mabini Reef, Malvar Reef, and Ayungin Shoal – areas which, under prevailing international law, are part of the Philippines' Exclusive Economic Zone and recognized by the United Nations Convention on the Law of the Sea.

There are many images that prove this reality, where even our own fishermen are driven away and prohibited from benefiting from the seas that rightfully belong to them. (...)

Today, we once again commemorate the long and bitter struggle to attain freedom.

At the time I made that speech – June 12, 2013 – our case against China's continuing illegal behavior was already being heard by the Permanent Court of Arbitration (PCA). The PCA's 2016 ruling would be a watershed moment for the Philippines. The tribunal invalidated China's nine-dash line claim and confirmed that features such as Panatag (Scarborough) Shoal and Panganibang (Mischief) Reef could not generate their own Exclusive Economic Zones (EEZ). China may have illegally occupied these and other features in the West Philippine Sea, but doing so did not give them any legal right to back up their spurious claim of "sovereignty" in the sea – a claim now dismissed by the court.

But now that the international legal situation had been so comprehensively resolved, it was essential to pass domestic legislation to implement the court's key rulings in Philippine law. For many years, across multiple congresses and administrations, the Philippines had attempted to pass comprehensive maritime zones legislation. Everyone agreed it was needed, but nobody had yet managed to push it across the finish line. I was determined to try.

In my early years as senator, I became increasingly vocal about Chinese aggression. I spoke about the water cannoning incidents, about the ramming of Philippine vessels, about Chinese underwater drones found in our waters, about espionage and the illegal building of artificial islands. The media helped expose these incidents, but within the Senate – modesty aside – I believe I was leading the charge.

My speeches attracted China's anger. My unwavering support for Philippine sovereignty made me a target. But I didn't care about China's approval; I cared about Philippine independence. I cared about Philippine rights, and the Philippine fishermen who could no longer safely fish in waters that had been theirs for generations. During the Covid 19 pandemic days, I helped the Philippine Navy develop Mavulis Island in the northernmost part of the Philippines, near Taiwan, into a naval base for the protection of Philippine sovereignty and so that our fishermen could shelter there during stormy weather conditions. That one action, perhaps more than any other, epitomizes the main concerns of my civil career: to ensure the wellbeing and security of all Filipinos, and to protect Philippine sovereignty.

(Author is shown visiting Mavulis Island with Philippne military officers)

Now, I felt that all of my experience in life – the legal training, the military education, the political experience, the personal connection to the Philippines as a whole and to these contested islands – was building toward something larger.

In the next phase of my Senate career, I would ask the Senate to create a special committee dedicated solely to these issues. I would shepherd two landmark laws through the legislative process against skepticism, delay and quiet opposition.

That story begins with the formation of the Special Committee on Philippine Maritime and Admiralty Zones, and the long fight to turn international law into Philippine law.

CHAPTER 9

Taking a Stand

Maritime zones bills had been filed in both the Philippine House and Senate across multiple Congresses, starting with the 15th Congress of 2010-2013, but none had made it through the full legislative process in either chamber. The bills would be filed, referred to committee … but would eventually come to nothing. In the 19th Congress, the House of Representatives succeeded in passing HB 7819 – the Philippine Maritime Zones Act – in May 2023. The Senate had never before successfully taken up maritime zones legislation. I sensed an historic opportunity. On July 25, 2023, I made what is called a "manifestation" to the Senate, proposing the creation of a special committee to single-mindedly address Philippine maritime zones and designated sea lanes for international shipping.

The very next day, July 26, 2023, the Senate Majority Leader in his capacity as Chairman of the Committee on Rules sponsored Senate Resolution 702 to create the Special Committee on Philippine Maritime and Admiralty Zones. In his sponsorship speech, he emphasized the urgency, stressing that we needed to clearly define our maritime boundaries to protect our sovereign interests, resources and people, and to prevent disputes with other nations. The Senate passed the resolution that same day.

There was no opposition, no delay and no political maneuvering; the ongoing crisis in the West Philippine Sea made the significance of the issue clear to everyone.

In the absence of proper maritime zones legislation, the Philippines had relied on the 2009 Republic Act No. 9522 which, as we saw in an earlier chapter, established our archipelagic baselines in compliance with the United Nations Convention on the Law of the Sea (UNCLOS). But baselines were just the beginning – the starting point from which we measure our territorial sea, our contiguous zone, our Exclusive Economic Zone (EEZ) and our continental shelf. Without a law declaring and defining these zones and specifying what rights we could exercise and legally enforce in each zone, the baselines were meaningless – like a foundation without a building.

On August 1, 2023, the Senate President designated me as chairman of the new committee. It was a powerful, cross-party group of senators – a signal that this was about the Philippines, not about politics.

My senatorial colleagues and I had our mandate. Now we had to deliver.

The Maritime Zones Act

The first organizational meeting and public hearing of the Special Committee took place on September 14, 2023, in the Senator Sotto Room at the Senate Financial Center. As chairman, I called the meeting to order and asked everyone to rise for a short prayer, followed by the singing of the national anthem. As the last echoes of the committee members' voices raised in patriotic song had faded away, I called for everyone to be seated, while I stayed on my feet to make my opening statement.

(Author is shown during the organizational meeting of the Senate Special Committee on Maritime and Admiralty Zones)

I saw that the doors to the committee room were closed, and I called out: *"OSSA [Office of the Seargeant-at-Arms], can you open the doors? We're holding a public hearing, but the doors are closed. Open them so we can be heard all the way to Scarborough Shoal!"*

It was perhaps a little theatrical on my part, but this was indeed supposed to be a public hearing, and calling for the doors to be thrown open was an important symbolic gesture. We were going to conduct this work transparently, so that China and the whole world could see what we were doing.

In my opening statement, I set out what we were trying to achieve:

"The Philippines are the second-largest archipelago in the world. With the constitution of this special committee and with the support of the other members of this body, this representation commits to ably steer the passage of bills that would not only reinforce our claims over disputed areas in the West Philippine Sea, but also harmonize our domestic legislation with the United Nations Convention on the Law of the Seas, improve our maritime governance, and help us maximize the blue economy. It is high time that we get our archipelagic house in order."

We had nine separate bills to consolidate, filed by various Senators. Each bill approached the issue from a slightly different angle, with different emphases and priorities. Our task was to take the best elements from all of them and craft a single, comprehensive piece of legislation.

Maritime law is extraordinarily complex, sitting at the intersection of international law, constitutional law, geography, marine science, and national security, so we assembled what I believe to have been one of the most impressive groups of experts ever brought together for a Philippine Senate committee. From the Philippine government, we had representatives from the Department of Foreign Affairs. From the Department of Justice came Attorney Fretti Ganchoon, whose expertise in the legal history of our maritime claims would prove invaluable. The Philippine Navy sent Captain Vincent J. Sibala. The National Mapping and Resource Information Authority provided Captain Carter S. Luma-Ang, whose technical knowledge of our baselines and maritime boundaries was essential. The National Intelligence Coordinating Agency and the National Security Council also sent representatives.

We also needed voices from outside government – academics and experts who could provide independent analysis and international perspective. Professor Jay Batongbacal from the University of the Philippines Institute for Maritime Affairs and Law of the Sea was crucial: Batongbacal had been studying these issues for years and understood both the technical details and the strategic implications better than almost anyone. We also brought in Dr. Stuart Kaye from the Australian National Centre on Ocean Resources and Security, Professor Gregory Poling from the Asia Maritime Transparency Initiative at the Center for Strategic and International Studies in Washington, and Professor Robert Beckman, Adjunct Senior Fellow in the Maritime Security Programme at the Institute for Defence and Strategic Studies of Nayang Technological University in Singapore.

These experts didn't just testify once and leave. Over the following weeks, they worked diligently with us in committee meetings to refine the language, address technical questions and ensure that what we were crafting would stand up to international scrutiny. We owe them a great debt of gratitude. I have personally expressed that gratitude to them on many occasions, and I do so again in these pages.

After some initial discussion of the nature and function of the committee and the swearing-in of our various "resource person" experts, I spelled out the economic stakes involved in our sovereignty over the West Philippine Sea.

I reminded the committee that the West Philippine Sea made up almost 40 percent of the total Philippine maritime domain, and supported at least some 370,000 fishermen, yet the total amount of fish harvested from this vast maritime domain accounted for only 6.36 percent of the total fisheries production of the country in 2022. The Philippines were forced to import fish from other countries, even as our own fish were poached from within our own EEZ.

I talked about rising electricity charges in the Philippines and the high proportion of the average Filipino household's income that was spent on electricity, and about how we were forced to import coal for our power stations – a highly polluting fuel, which exacerbates the impact of climate change, resulting in more frequent and more powerful typhoons. And yet, at the same time, the vast energy resources in the West Philippine Sea remained untapped, with Recto Bank alone estimated to contain millions of barrels of oil and trillions of cubic feet of natural gas.

"Leaving the Philippines maritime zones largely undefined," I argued, "will slow our ability to responsibly exploit and develop our resources. How can Filipinos properly enjoy the bounties of the ocean and manage the same if we don't have maritime zones? It is high time that we walk our talk; not just [to] align ourselves with the UN Convention on the Law of the Sea, and the final and binding 2016 arbitral ruling, but to allow Filipinos to responsibly enjoy the bounty of the Philippines' rich maritime and archipelagic waters."

After that first meeting, the Committee continued with its painstaking work. Three months later, in late November 2023, the bill received its second reading on the floor of the Senate. I delivered a strong sponsorship speech. I have taken the liberty of quoting that speech here in full, because, to this day, it encapsulates perfectly my thinking and the drive behind my passionate belief in the bill's importance.

Mr. President, dear colleagues of this august chamber, the Senate Special Committee on Philippine Maritime and Admiralty Zones is honored to sponsor Senate Bill No. 2492 or the Philippine Maritime Zones Act of 2023 (...)

I stand before you to emphasize the crucial significance of Maritime Zones Law in the Philippines as an archipelagic nation with a vast expanse of waters. Understanding and upholding the Maritime Zones Law is not merely a legal obligation but a paramount necessity for our nation's security, economic prosperity, and environmental well-being.

The Maritime Zones Law delineates the boundaries that define our sovereign rights and jurisdiction over the surrounding seas. The Philippines' exclusive economic zone and territorial waters are not just lines on a map; they are the lifeblood of our maritime activities. They provide us with exclusive rights to exploit and manage marine resources, including fisheries, minerals, and energy.

After three Congresses, the Senate is finally able to move this foundational bill to the plenary session.

Allow me to begin with the premise that binds us Filipinos – the Philippines are an archipelagic and maritime nation. With a total of 7,641 islands, we are the second largest archipelago in the world. More than 62% of the country's municipalities and cities thrive on our coasts. Many of us rely on the bounty of our seas for food.

In 2020, there was a Food and Nutrition Research Institute (DOST-FNRI) report stating that fish consumption is 14 kilogram per individual per year and comprises about 40% of the total animal-sourced protein consumed by Filipinos. We have a long tradition of living and working at sea; not only do our waters contribute significantly to our food and economic security – our seas, our oceans are an integral component to our identity as Filipinos.

With all the wealth from our waters – both in terms of culture and natural resources, we are obliged to have the collective responsibility to uphold, sustainably harness, and protect our maritime domain.

The fundamental interests of the Philippines are inextricably linked to its waters. This necessitates and underscores the importance of having effective maritime governance. At its core lies the clear identification of the maritime areas over which the Philippines exercises sovereignty, control, or sovereign rights and jurisdiction, and of the specific legal powers that the Philippines would exercise in those areas.

Our Constitution has bestowed upon this august body the task to safeguard national interest by ensuring that the necessary laws and policies are in place for the State, and I quote, "To protect the nation's marine wealth in its archipelagic waters, territorial sea, and exclusive economic zone, and reserve its use and enjoyment exclusively to Filipino citizens." The Committee, therefore, cannot overemphasize enough that the adoption of this measure is not only critical and imperative, but also very timely and necessary. (...)

The United Nations Convention on the Law of the Sea or UNCLOS governs the allocation of maritime areas and the states' rights, entitlements, and responsibilities over these.

It has been more than 41 years since UNCLOS was adopted, and as a party to the convention, the Philippines are duty-bound and legally-bound to exercise its entitlements, perform its treaty obligations, and ensure that our domestic laws are in harmony with the provisions of UNCLOS.

In 1998, the Philippines also declared that it "intends to harmonize its domestic legislation with the provisions of the Convention," and I am referring to UNCLOS.

In 2009, the Philippines made the first significant step through the enactment of Republic Act 9522, which made the baselines of the Philippines fully compliant with UNCLOS.

The Supreme Court declared in the case of Magallona vs Executive Secretary, *that, "The enactment of UNCLOS-compliant baselines law for the Philippine archipelago and adjacent areas, as embodied in RA 9522, allows an internationally recognized delimitation of the breadth of the Philippines' maritime zones and continental shelf."*

After the passage of the baselines law, the next logical step for the Philippines to take is to enact a law that will establish with certainty our territorial sea, contiguous zone, Exclusive Economic Zone (EEZ), and our continental shelf and allow us to further understand and exercise our rights and obligations in each zone as underscored by UNCLOS and other relevant laws.

The Philippine Maritime Zones Act will enable the Philippines to fully enforce applicable maritime laws and enjoy its rights over its territory and exclusive economic zone and pave the way for clarifying and updating relevant maritime laws and policies which have been enacted prior to UNCLOS. This will further fortify our rights and entitlements over our maritime zones and provide the country with a strong diplomatic negotiating tool in pursuing our interests therein.

In addition to this, the clear delineation of the maritime boundaries of the Philippines will help relevant government institutions in harnessing ocean resources and maritime spaces that are crucial in developing the country's blue economy potential.

According to a study by Dr. Rhodora Azanza, the blue economy potential of the Philippines, using 2007 prices, is pegged at US$966 billion to US$1.5 trillion if the continental shelf is included.

In sum, the Maritime Zones Law will help the Philippines in numerous ways and can even serve as a foundational policy that: (1) serves as the driving force for the Philippines to forge a comprehensive maritime security framework, (2) advances the Philippine interest most especially in terms of protecting, sustainably harnessing, and maximizing the Philippines' marine resources, (3) provides guidance on the rights, duties, and entitlements of the Philippines on different maritime zones, and (4) finally, be utilized to further the goals of other relevant maritime laws of the Philippines.

One of our predecessors had the distinct honor of serving as the country's lead negotiator when the Law of the Sea was being debated by the United Nations. Senator Arturo Tolentino left all of us a message when he spoke at the 189th Plenary meeting of the Third United Nations Conference on the Law of the Sea in 1982. Senator Tolentino told us that the UNCLOS is a "historic milestone in the progressive development of international law, a monumental achievement of cooperation and goodwill among nations. Its provisions, many of them introducing new concepts, will govern the seas and the resources of the world for generations to come, even long after the individuals who participated in the Conference are long gone and forgotten."

It is now our turn to continue the work of Senator Tolentino by adopting one of the most important laws in our country's history. The Philippine Maritime Zones Act of 2023 will be inscribed as a pivotal moment in our maritime history. It is now the time for Congress, particularly the Senate of the Philippines, to stand up for what is ours and take this fundamental step in ensuring that our national interests in Philippine waters are protected, by passing this law that will "govern the seas and resources of the Philippines for generations to come."

May I just also remind my dear colleagues of the many incidents of aggression from our Chinese counterparts that we have experienced recently in the West Philippine Sea. One too many incidents of aggression already. It is time we take a stand against this bullying. With the passage of this Maritime Zones Act, Mr. President, we are taking a firm stand.

Several of my fellow Senators then made important speeches of co-sponsorship of the bill.

Senator Loren Lagarda spoke about "illegal, unreported and unregulated" (IUU) fishing, piracy and territorial disputes, and about how the bill would "strengthen our country's position as a responsible coastal and archipelagic state that adheres to international law."

Senator Zubiri spoke of the many incursions into the West Philippine Sea by "a superpower with far greater military might" and of the need to establish our territory not only in the interests of defense and security, but also to safeguard our maritime resources and to allow further maritime research.

Senator Gatchalian spoke of the need to reaffirm our sovereign rights and, again, to preserve our maritime environment and conduct marine scientific research.

To this day, I am more grateful than I can say for the support of my fellow senators in the work of drafting the Maritime Zones Act.

The floor debates continued on December 4, 2023, against a backdrop of renewed Chinese aggression that made our work feel even more urgent and necessary. In the weeks before I rose to defend the Act on the Senate floor, large numbers of Chinese maritime militia vessels had been swarming Julian Felipe (Whitsun) Reef in the Kalayaan Island Group – well within the Philippines' EEZ. The fleet of militia vessels eventually grew to one hundred and thirty-five. The tactic of "swarming" had begun in 2021, also on Julian Felipe Reef, when around 220 Chinese militia vessels were involved, claiming they were sheltering from bad weather, even though the weather was good. It was a classic technique, allowing China to harass and deny access to other shipping while maintaining strategic deniability of any wrongdoing under the guise of "ordinary fishing activities" – even when, according to *Rappler*, there was no reported evidence of the militia vessels carrying out any "actual fishing activities."[98]

(Author is shown explaining the importance of UNCLOS on the Philippine Senate floor)

With Christmas only eight days away, we were about to send the traditional Christmas convoy to resupply troops garrisoned on the BRP *Sierra Madre* at Ayungin (Second Thomas) Shoal. With the swarm of Chinese militia vessels at Julian Felipe Reef, a mere 54 nautical miles from Ayungin Shoal, it raised the question, as I pointed out to the committee, as to whether we would be allowed to deliver Christmas gifts to our Philippine Navy troops on board the *Sierra Madre*. As we debated maritime law, our sailors and fishermen faced the reality of Chinese aggression. Every parliamentary procedure, every technical amendment, every legal definition we discussed had immediate, tangible consequences for Filipinos at sea.

I did not believe that the morning's news about the vessels swarming Julian Felipe Reef was a coincidence – it was part of a pattern of escalating Chinese behavior designed to persuade us to abandon our efforts to enshrine the judgements of the Permanent Court of Arbitration's ruling on UNCLOS into Philippine law. We were determined not to be intimidated.

In this December 4th debate, one senator addressed the house to raise a fundamental question: "Why is it necessary to enact the Maritime Zones Law?" This was my cue to deliver a clear and compelling argument.

I offered three core reasons. Firstly, the essential legal clarity needed to provide a foundation for maritime governance and law enforcement. Secondly – and of vital importance – it gave *practical* clarity to our administrative and enforcement agencies, specifically the National Mapping and Resource Information Authority, the Philippine Navy, the Philippine Coast Guard, the Philippine National Police Maritime Group, and the Bureau of

Fisheries and Aquatic Resources. It would be clear, for the first time, within exactly which boundaries these agencies should operate. “Any doubts remaining as to the location and nature of enforcement will be removed once and for all,” I said. “It will be clarified where the boundaries of our reefs are, where the boundaries of our shoals are, where the boundaries of our islands are.” The third reason was equally vital. "A Maritime Zones Law will ensure that the Philippines asserts and exercises sovereign rights of the Philippines not only over its legal 200-nautical-mile continental shelf but also lays the basis for the extended continental shelf beyond 200 nautical miles (…) It will put other states, other countries on notice that no foreign entity or person can explore or exploit the gas mineral resources in our seabed without the express authorization of the Philippine Government and subject to compliance with our own laws and regulations."

I reminded my colleagues that China was trying to undermine the validity of the rights granted to us by UNCLOS precisely by questioning why we had not passed these into Philippine law. I argued that if we were able to pass the law and China continued to harass us afterward, then they would be in clear breach of our laws and could no longer throw doubt on our rights by saying they were “only stated in UNCLOS.”

I wanted to be realistic with my colleagues about what the law could and couldn't do. "A law cannot prevent a violator from transgressing the law," I said, drawing a parallel to the terrible bombing that had occurred the previous day at Mindanao State University, when Islamist terrorists bombed a Catholic Mass being held in the university’s gymnasium. There are, of course, laws that prohibit such terrorist attacks, I argued, but if there are bad people who are determined to carry out such acts, they will still go ahead. It was the same with the new Act, I reasoned: even when we have a law, if there are still those who want to violate it – as the People's Republic of China was doing and might continue to do – we might not be able to stop them. But our claim against them would become stronger.

One of the most important exchanges of the day came when a senator asked about the territory of Sabah (North Borneo) – a question that touched on one of the most sensitive issues in Philippine foreign policy. Our claim to Sabah is historical and longstanding, predating even our independence. Would defining our maritime zones somehow undermine that territorial claim?

I had to be precise in my answer, because this was exactly the kind of constitutional concern that had derailed previous attempts at maritime legislation.

"Mr. President, let me explain," I said. "Our Maritime Zone Law is anchored literally on UNCLOS – United Nations Convention on the Law of the Seas. We, likewise, incorporated in the measure the implications of the 2016 Arbitral Ruling. To clarify, our claim, our Maritime Zones Law, is about UNCLOS. UNCLOS deals only with waters – ocean, seas, waters, rivers, et cetera, et cetera. Our claim regarding Sabah is about land; it is about territory.

"UNCLOS does not settle territorial or sovereignty disputes between states. (…) It provides and regulates the drawing of maritime zones from the state's baselines. (...) Even the Dispute Settlement Mechanism under UNCLOS is limited to the interpretation or application of the convention of UNCLOS, which, again, I reiterate, refers to waters, oceans, seas, rivers, base, archipelago, et cetera, et cetera."

I quoted directly from the 2016 Arbitral Tribunal ruling: "The Tribunal noted, and I quote: 'UNCLOS does not address the sovereignty of states over land territory.' Thus, the Maritime Zones Act will not have any effect, direct or indirect, on the Philippines' claim to Sabah, in the same way that UNCLOS does not have an effect on the claim."

We were securing our maritime rights without compromising our territorial claims. The two existed in separate legal frameworks and did not interfere with each other.

The debates continued into the New Year, until March 2024.

There were no political battles, no partisan divisions, no senators positioning themselves as opponents of the bill. What we had instead was a careful, collaborative process of refinement. In February, we entered the period of individual amendments raised by various of my colleagues: sharpening definitions, clarifying jurisdictions, ensuring that every technical detail was correct. For every proposed amendment, my response was the same: "We accept the motion." "We agree." "We find it very consistent with the previous provisions." "We accept the proposal." Once the amendments had been proposed and discussed, the presiding officer would ask: "Is there any objection?" The response would be silence, and the officer would say: "There being none, the amendment is approved."

This was legislation built on expert consensus and national necessity, not political positioning. Every senator who engaged with the bill did so constructively, recognizing that this was about the Philippines versus external threats, not about political parties pitted against each other.

Senate Bill 2492, the Philippine Maritime Zones Act, formally passed the Senate on February 26, 2024, with a unanimous vote of 23-0-0. It was passed by the House of Representatives on May 29, and the House ratified the consolidated bicameral conference committee report – a standard procedure when the two chambers pass different versions of the same bill – on August 20, 2024. I would like to take this opportunity to thank Representative Rachel Arenas for her help in that.

After years of failure across many Congresses, after fifteen months of intensive work, countless hours of expert testimony and technical refinement, the Philippine Maritime Zones Act was approved.

The Archipelagic Sea Lanes Act

The Maritime Zones Act defined *where* our sovereignty extended. But there was another question that needed answering: *how* would foreign vessels move through our archipelagic waters?

This was not a theoretical concern. The Philippines are the world's second-largest archipelago. Every day, huge volumes of international shipping passes through our seas – both commercial and military vessels. Aircraft fly overhead. Under international law, they have certain rights of passage.

But under that same international law, we have the right to regulate *where* that passage occurs.

Article 53 of the UNCLOS is explicit: "An archipelagic state may designate sea lanes and air routes thereabove, suitable for the continuous and expeditious passage of foreign ships and aircraft through or over its archipelagic waters and the adjacent territorial sea."

May designate. Not must. Not shall. May.

For decades, we hadn't exercised that right. Foreign vessels moved through Philippine waters as they chose, following routes that may or may not have aligned with Philippine interests. We had no legal framework to channel that traffic through designated corridors, no way to ensure that sensitive areas were protected, or to assert that while we respected innocent right of passage, we had the right to determine exactly *where* that passage should be.

A perfect example of the need for such legislation had occurred in 2022, when a Chinese People's Liberation Army Navy (PLAN) *Dongdiao*-class electronic reconnaissance ship, PLAN 792, entered the Sulu Sea, in the southwest of the Philippines, without permission. The Sulu Sea, which lies between Mindanao and Palawan, was the location for the Philippine-US Marine Exercise 2022 (MAREX 22), which the Chinese vessel was clearly monitoring. PLAN 72 was repeatedly challenged by BRP *Antonio Luna*, and ordered to leave, but the Chinese vessel claimed it was exercising its right of innocent passage. The Philippine Department of Foreign Affairs (DFA) disagreed, protesting about the ship's "illegal intrusion and lingering presence" in Philippine waters. "The actions of PLAN 792 did not constitute innocent passage and violated Philippine sovereignty," the DFA said, announcing that it had summoned the Chinese Ambassador to explain the incident.[99]

The Archipelagic Sea Lanes Act would establish the framework that would make such incidents a clear violation of Philippine law. The Act would be the twin law to the Maritime Zones Act – two pieces of complementary legislation that would create a comprehensive legal architecture for Philippine maritime governance. While I had been shepherding the Maritime Zones Act through the Senate, I had also been working on this second measure. They moved through the legislative process on parallel tracks, though the Archipelagic Sea Lanes Act followed a slightly different timeline.

The work began in earnest in January 2024, as the Maritime Zones Act was still in its final stages of debate and amendment. On January 24, 2024, the Special Committee on Philippine Maritime and Admiralty Zones held its first public hearing specifically on the Archipelagic Sea Lanes Act.

As with the Maritime Zones Act, we were consolidating multiple bills. Various other Senators had all filed versions of the legislation; each approached the issue from slightly different angles, with different emphases. Our task, once more, was to take the best elements from all these bills and craft a single, coherent piece of legislation.

Again, we assembled expert resource persons to help us get the technical details right. Secretary Enrique Manalo from the Department of Foreign Affairs was there, bringing the diplomatic perspective. The Department of National Defense sent representatives. The National Security

Council was present, along with the National Intelligence Coordinating Agency. The Philippine Coastguard, the Department of Justice, The University of the Philippines' Institute for Maritime and Affairs and the Law of Sea all sent representatives – anyone whose agency or institution had a bearing on the bill was present to contribute to the discussions and make their voices heard. Professors Stuart Kaye from the Australian National Centre on Ocean Resources and Security, and Robert Beckman from the Maritime Security Programme at the Institute for Defense and Strategic Studies in Singapore, also joined these committee hearings.

We needed to ensure that the sea lanes we designated would work practically – that they harmonized with international law and would neither disrupt legitimate international commerce nor compromise Philippine security or environmental protection.

The hearings continued until April. The fundamental concept was straightforward: we would designate three specific sea lanes connecting various points across the archipelago. These would become the legally recognized routes for foreign vessels exercising their right of archipelagic sea lanes passage.

These were not arbitrary lines on a map. They were carefully considered corridors that balanced international navigation rights with Philippine sovereignty, security, and environmental concerns. They provided foreign vessels with reasonable routes for passage while ensuring that vast areas of our archipelagic waters remained under exclusive Philippine jurisdiction for our own use.

On May 13, 2024, I stood before the Senate to deliver the sponsorship speech for Senate Bill No. 2665: the Philippine Archipelagic Sea Lanes Act.

"Madam President," I began (at this point, Senate President Zubiri had relinquished the chair to President Pro Tempore Legarda). "The bill will establish a system of sea lanes in the Philippine waters by connecting the coordinates of the following axis lines;

a) Philippine Sea - Balintang Channel - West Philippine Sea;

b) Celebes Sea - Sibutu Passage - Sulu Sea - Cuyo East Pass - Mindoro Strait - West Philippine Sea;

c) Celebes Sea - Basilan Strait - Sulu Sea - Nasubata Channel – Balabac Strait - West Philippine Sea.

"We need these archipelagic sea lanes. Madam President, because we are made up of so many islands – 7,641 islands. The international community afforded us the right to do so. We have earned our legal and international recognition in no less than the UN Convention on the Law of the Sea (UNCLOS).

"Article 53 (1) of UNCLOS states: 'an archipelagic state may designate sea lanes and air routes thereabove, suitable for the continuous and expeditious passage of foreign ships and aircraft through or over its archipelagic waters and the adjacent territorial sea.'

"But we need an enabling law. We need this for our national security; we need this for jurisdictional clarity; and we need this for resource management.

"Madam President, on behalf of all our brave men and women patrolling the West Philippine Sea, on behalf of our fishermen being deprived of their fishing rights in Scarborough Shoal, and on behalf of our maritime nation that needs reinforced legal protection, I call on each of our colleagues here to likewise see the urgency of this measure and prioritize the immediate passage of this bill."

I quoted Article 53 directly, emphasizing that key word: *may.* This was a right we were choosing to exercise, not an obligation imposed upon us. By designating these sea lanes, we were asserting Philippine sovereignty while remaining fully compliant with international law.

Senator Lagarda delivered a co-sponsorship speech which highlighted the protections the Act would guarantee. "The designation of archipelagic sea lanes solidifies our sovereignty and our maritime domain," said Lagarda. "It prevents unwanted and arbitrary passage of foreign vessels. This is important because the breach of such threatens and harms our marine ecosystem and biodiversity, our national sovereignty, and the security of Philippine flag vessels. This Act prevents foreign vessels from polluting, conducting research and survey activities, fishing, marine bioprospecting, and loading and unloading of persons, goods, or currency."

Another senator talked eloquently about Filipino fishermen being driven forcibly from their traditional fishing spots within our own EEZ and deprived of their livelihoods. "The establishment of Philippine Archipelagic Sea Lanes as embodied in the proposed bill will ensure the protection of fishing grounds and key biodiversity areas in Philippine waters," he said. "This will safeguard the integrity of our national territory. Further, the proposed measure ensures that foreign ships and aircraft exercising the right of archipelagic sea lanes shall not engage in threat or use of force against the sovereignty, territorial integrity, or political independence of the Republic of the Philippines or in any other manner in violation of the principles of international law embodied in the Charter of the United Nations."

Senator Gatchalian echoed these points and drew a strong conclusion: "The Philippine Archipelagic Sea Lanes Act is a bold step forward." said Gatchalian. "It is a declaration of our resolve to protect our maritime heritage, a blueprint for sustainable development, and a framework for peaceful and cooperative use of our archipelagic waters."

The floor debates on the Archipelagic Sea Lanes Act followed a similar pattern to those on the Maritime Zones Act. There was no partisan opposition, no political grandstanding. What we had instead was careful, technical scrutiny.

The debates continued through July and August 2024.

Throughout this period, senators again proposed amendments – technical refinements to improve the clarity of the language, to ensure proper coordination with existing laws, to specify enforcement mechanisms. As with the Maritime Zones Act, these were collaborative improvements, not adversarial attacks.

The process demonstrated what the Philippine Senate can accomplish when legislators set aside partisan politics and focus on national interest. Senators from different parties, with different political backgrounds, working together because they recognized that maritime sovereignty transcends political affiliation. Senate Minority Leader Koko Pimentel deserves special mention for his help in crafting and passing both bills.

On August 13, 2024, the Senate approved the bill by a unanimous 22-0-0 vote. By September 4, 2024, both the Senate and the House of Representatives had passed their versions of the Archipelagic Sea Lanes Act. A conference committee met, as with the Maritime Zones Act, to reconcile any differences in the two bills. On September 4, 2024, the Senate approved the conference committee report. The Archipelagic Sea Lanes Act had passed.

Like the Maritime Zones Act, it now awaited the President's signature to become law.

Standing together, the Maritime Zones Act and the Archipelagic Sea Lanes Act represented the most comprehensive assertion of Philippine maritime sovereignty in our nation's history.

The Maritime Zones Act declared, with the force of domestic law, exactly where our territorial sea, contiguous zone, EEZ and continental shelf began and ended. It specified what rights we could exercise in each zone and what enforcement powers our agencies possessed. It took the 2016 Arbitral Tribunal ruling – which China had dismissed – and domesticated it into Philippine law, giving it teeth.

The Archipelagic Sea Lanes Act complemented this by regulating how foreign vessels would move through our archipelagic waters. It respected international rights of passage while asserting Philippine authority to designate where that passage would occur. It said to the world: yes, you may transit through our waters, but you will do so on routes that we have designated, in accordance with rules that we have established, in recognition of our sovereignty as an archipelagic state.

Together, these laws meant that for the first time since independence, the Philippines had a complete legal framework for maritime governance – one that was consistent with international law, grounded in our Constitution, validated by international tribunals, and enforceable by our institutions.

But there was still one more hurdle to clear.

What happened next was one of the most frustrating periods of my legislative career – a test of patience that lasted months and revealed the complex and sometimes opaque intersection between the legislative and executive branches of government.

The Senate had passed the bill. The House of Representatives had passed their version. The bicameral conference committee had reconciled the two versions. All that remained was for President Marcos to sign it into law.

For weeks, nothing seemed to happen. Other bills, some that had been enrolled after the Maritime Zones Act, were being signed and passed into law. I couldn't understand it. This was arguably one of the most important pieces of legislation the Senate had passed in years. It addressed a crisis that was happening in real time, with Chinese vessels swarming our waters and harassing our fishermen. Every day of delay was a day that we couldn't fully implement our maritime sovereignty.

There were sleepless nights. Long conversations with colleagues and friends, trying to understand what was happening and why. The frustration built as the delays continued with no clear explanation.

I won't claim to know for certain what caused the delay. I began to worry that some sort of pressure was being applied behind the scenes – perhaps business interests that were keen not to upset their relations with China, or the ever-present faction of those who believed it was best not to provoke Beijing. What I do know is that the delay was real, the frustration was intense, and the relief when the bill was finally signed was profound.

The Maritime Zones Act became Republic Act No. 12064. The Archipelagic Sea Lanes Act – the twin law that we had shepherded through a similar process – became Republic Act No. 12065. Together, they represented the most significant advancement in Philippine maritime law in decades.

After decades of trying, we had finally put our archipelagic house in order.

CHAPTER 10

Securing Our Sovereignty

My two landmark pieces of legislation, Republic Act No. 12064, or the Philippine Maritime Zones Act, and Republic Act No. 12065, or the Philippine Archipelagic Sea Lanes Act, are technical in nature, deeply political, historical, and nationalistic.

These laws are not just statutes, but living testaments to our determination to protect the patrimony entrusted to us by our forefathers, and to secure our sovereignty for our future generations.

The Philippines, as an archipelagic state of over seven thousand islands, is bound together by waters that serve both as our lifelines and our frontiers. These waters form part of critical international sea lanes and sustain an ecosystem abundant with marine biodiversity, coral reefs, and vast energy resources beneath the seabed. Our geography is both a blessing and a challenge – a source of life, livelihood, and identity, yet also a frontier of vulnerability in an increasingly complex maritime domain.

For many decades, however, the Philippines faced a persistent gap between the maritime rights recognized under international law and the domestic mechanisms required to enforce them. While the United Nations

Convention on the Law of the Sea (UNCLOS) provided the legal architecture for our entitlements, our national legislation lagged behind, creating uncertainty in the protection and utilization of our maritime zones.

The Philippine Maritime Zones Act and the Philippine Archipelagic Sea Lanes Act emerged from this necessity – a necessity shaped by national security imperatives, economic aspirations, and environmental stewardship. They were enacted in response to the realities of the West Philippine Sea, where the rule of law is continually tested by assertions of might and unilateral actions.

Guided by the 2016 Arbitral Award in Philippines v. China and grounded on UNCLOS, these statutes harmonize our domestic legal framework with our international commitments. Together, they reinforce our maritime entitlements, provide legal certainty to our navy, coast guard and enforcement agencies, and affirm that the Philippines will defend its sovereignty not through provocation, but through precision – by ensuring that the law of the sea remains the law of nations.

To secure the West Philippine Sea is to secure our national future. Control, in this sense, is not about domination but stewardship; the capacity to govern our seas under the rule of law, to protect their resources for our people, and to ensure that our maritime destiny is determined not by external forces, but by the sovereign will of the Filipino nation. Our maritime laws are not merely statutes. They are living testaments to our sovereignty – a peaceful assertion that, in the community of nations, law, not force, defines the boundaries of our seas.

The Philippine Maritime Zones Act, signed into law on November 7, 2024, represents the Philippines' long-awaited effort to translate international law into domestic statute – to operationalize what the 1982 United Nations Convention on the Law of the Sea (UNCLOS) and the 2016 Arbitral Award had already affirmed: that our maritime rights are defined by law, not by force, and that our sovereignty extends not by conquest, but by the rule of law.

The Act adopts Article 76 of UNCLOS, defining the continental shelf as the natural prolongation of the land territory to the outer edge of the continental margin, or up to 200 nautical miles where the margin does not reach that distance.

It further recognizes the Talampas ng Pilipinas, or Benham Rise, as part of the Philippine Extended Continental Shelf, consistent with the recommendation of the UN Commission on the Limits of the Continental Shelf (CLCS) in 2012.

This provision secures sovereign rights over the minerals, petroleum, and sedentary species found on and beneath the seabed – rights explicitly granted under Articles 77 to 81 of UNCLOS. What once was merely a scientific discovery (the underwater plateau east of Luzon was discovered in discovered in 1933 by American surveyor Andrew Ellicott Kennedy Benham) is now enshrined in statute, transforming Benham Rise from an academic subject into a national asset – Benham Rise is thought to hold significant hydrocarbon reserves.

The law subjects marine scientific research within Philippine jurisdiction to Part XIII of UNCLOS, requiring prior consent of the coastal state. At the same time, it mandates protection and preservation of the marine environment, consistent with Part XII of the Convention. This alignment ensures that our development of our marine resources is governed by sustainability and stewardship, not exploitation – an echo of UNCLOS' dual commitment to both progress and preservation.

The Act acknowledges that, where Philippine maritime zones overlap with those of neighboring states, boundaries must be determined by agreement, in accordance with Article 74 and Article 83 of UNCLOS. If unresolved, disputes shall be settled peacefully under Part XV, the very process that enabled the 2016 arbitration against China. This provision institutionalizes our commitment to peaceful resolution of maritime disputes, ensuring that diplomacy and dialogue remain the first resort.

Finally, the Act requires that the Philippines exercise its maritime rights with due regard for the rights and duties of other states – a principle anchored in Articles 56 and 58 of UNCLOS. This clause reflects our recognition that while sovereignty entails rights, it also imposes responsibilities.

Our assertion of jurisdiction must always be tempered by the rule of law, mutual respect, and international cooperation. The Act is therefore not merely a restatement of UNCLOS – it is its domestication. It translates the treaty's geographic framework and legal architecture into an enforceable national statute. It provides the legal muscle by which Philippine courts, law enforcement agencies, and diplomatic missions can act with precision and legitimacy. In doing so, it gives domestic effect to the 2016 Arbitral Award, strengthens our capacity to manage marine resources, and provides a legal basis for future negotiations and boundary settlements.

In both structure and spirit, the Act faithfully mirrors UNCLOS.

It consolidates our maritime entitlements, enhances our enforcement posture, and reinforces the Philippines' role as a steadfast advocate of a rules-based maritime order in the Indo-Pacific.

A maritime law, no matter how eloquent, must ultimately live in enforcement. The Philippine Maritime Zones Act provides not only a definition of our maritime domains, but more importantly, a statutory foundation for asserting and defending them.

By domesticating the principles of UNCLOS and the 2016 Arbitral Award, this law transforms our maritime rights from abstract entitlements into operational mandates – actionable, defensible, and enforceable under Philippine and international law.

Before the Act, our enforcement agencies operated under fragmented statutes – fisheries laws, environmental codes, and naval regulations – each asserting jurisdiction but without a unified legal framework. the Act aligns our domestic law with UNCLOS – the very instrument that governs maritime zones worldwide.

This legal clarity is crucial. It leaves no ambiguity about where Philippine jurisdiction begins and ends. It allows our enforcement agencies – from the Philippine Coast Guard to the Navy, from the Bureau of Fisheries and Agriculture to the Department of Environmental and Natural Resources – to act with certainty and legitimacy. Every interception, arrest, or enforcement action now rests on a solid statutory basis, eliminating room for diplomatic dispute or legal contestation.

By defining and asserting our maritime zones, the Act strengthens the legal backbone of our sovereignty and sovereign rights. It provides the statutory authority for our government to act against incursions – whether by foreign fishing fleets, unauthorized survey vessels, or illegal drilling operations – within our EEZ and continental shelf.

These international principles are now domestically codified. They can be invoked not only in international fora, but before Philippine courts and agencies. This transforms what was once an arbitral declaration into a living mandate for national enforcement.

The Act also enhances our enforcement posture by providing a legal basis for resource allocation and inter-agency coordination.

It justifies greater investment in maritime patrol assets, surveillance technology, and operational logistics. Our Coast Guard and Navy can now secure additional funding not merely on security grounds, but on the explicit statutory obligation to patrol and protect the maritime zones defined by law.

It establishes a framework for inter-agency coordination. The law clarifies the complementary roles of the Philippine Navy, Philippine Coast Guard, Bureau of Fisheries and Aquatic Resources (BFAR), Philippine National Police Maritime Group, and other relevant agencies. This ensures that our maritime enforcement is integrated, not overlapping – that we act as one state, under one legal mandate.

Finally, it strengthens deterrence. By prescribing penalties for violations such as illegal fishing, unauthorized exploration, pollution, and illegal marine scientific research, the law sends a clear signal: that the Philippines has both the will and the legal means to protect its waters.

But enforcement is not only about defense; it is also about protection – of resources, livelihoods, and ecosystems. The Act enables the Philippines to safeguard its natural resources by clearly identifying where our EEZ and continental shelf lie. This allows us to act decisively against illegal, unreported, and unregulated (IUU) fishing, and to prevent unauthorized energy exploration or marine exploitation.

Such protection ensures that the benefits of our seas flow to our own people – to the Filipino fisherfolk in Masinloc, Palawan, or Pangasinan – and not to foreign entities operating in violation of international law.

The law also mandates the protection and preservation of the marine environment. It empowers government agencies to prevent pollution, habitat destruction and other activities that threaten our marine biodiversity – directly implementing the environmental obligations of Articles 192 to 194 of UNCLOS. The Act strengthens both economic security and environmental sustainability, making enforcement a tool for national resilience.

In diplomatic terms, the law serves as a legal shield – a codified expression of national resolve. It transforms our legal arguments into statutory policy, giving our diplomats, lawyers, and defense officials a clear legislative mandate when engaging in regional and international dialogue. In doing so, the Philippines reaffirms its role as a law-abiding maritime nation and a champion of a rules-based order in the Indo-Pacific.

The Arbitral Award of 2016, while binding, is not self-executing. It required domestic implementation. The Act provides precisely that mechanism – a national legal instrument that empowers Philippine agencies and courts to enforce the rights recognized internationally. It ensures that the Philippines can respond legally and diplomatically to violations, backed by both international legitimacy and domestic authority. It turns maritime law into maritime power – not through force, but through lawful capability. It gives our law enforcement agencies a clear map of jurisdiction, our courts a legal basis for adjudication, and our diplomats a foundation for negotiation. It reinforces sovereignty, strengthens deterrence, and promotes economic and ecological security – all within the boundaries of international law.

Through the Act – R.A. 12064 – the Philippines has fortified its position as a nation that governs its seas by the compass of law, not by the tides of politics. It ensures that every patrol, every enforcement action, and every diplomatic note stands on firm legal ground – on the same principles recognized by UNCLOS and vindicated by the 2016 Arbitral Award.

In the words of principle, not passion: our maritime sovereignty is now codified, operationalized, and enforceable.

The passage of the Philippine Archipelagic Sea Lanes Act, or Republic Act No. 12065, in November 2024, marks another milestone in the continuing evolution of our maritime legal framework.

At its core, R.A. 12065 was enacted to formalize and regulate the passage of foreign vessels and aircraft through the Philippines' archipelagic waters.

This was a long-overdue step – one that closed a critical legal gap that had persisted for decades. Before this law, the Philippines had yet to designate specific Archipelagic Sea Lanes (ASLs), as authorized by Article 53 of UNCLOS. In the absence of such designation, foreign vessels could claim the right to traverse any route "normally used for international navigation" through our waters – a loophole that left our archipelagic sovereignty vulnerable to exploitation.

R.A. 12065 ends that ambiguity.

It draws clear lines on the map, prescribing designated routes through which foreign ships and aircraft may pass, and defining what they may – and may not – do while in transit. By designating specific ASLs, the law distinguishes archipelagic sea lanes passage from the broader freedom of navigation that applies on the high seas. This distinction is vital.

Under UNCLOS, archipelagic waters are sovereign waters of the archipelagic state. Foreign vessels do not enjoy unfettered movement; they are entitled only to continuous, expeditious, and unobstructed passage along routes designated by the archipelagic state itself. R.A. 12065 affirms that while we recognize navigational rights, they operate within Philippine sovereignty, not against it.

The law also enumerates explicit obligations for foreign ships and aircraft transiting through the ASLs. They must pass as quickly and directly as possible, without unnecessary delay or deviation; refrain from activities prejudicial to Philippine peace, order, or security, including war games, military exercises, or intelligence operations; avoid pollution, unauthorized research, or fishing; and keep their Automatic Identification Systems (AIS) and communication equipment active and responsive to Philippine authorities.

These obligations ensure that foreign passage remains transparent, non-threatening, and compliant with international norms. They also reinforce the Philippines' environmental jurisdiction within its archipelagic waters, prohibiting harmful practices such as marine bioprospecting or dumping of waste.

Importantly, the law demonstrates that the Philippines are both a sovereign state and a responsible member of the international community. By establishing archipelagic sea lanes, we fulfill our obligation under UNCLOS to facilitate safe and orderly transit, while ensuring that such passage does not compromise national security or marine protection. In this sense, the Act strikes the delicate balance between navigational freedom and sovereign control – the essence of the archipelagic principle.

Beyond its legal purpose, the Archipelagic Sea Lanes Act carries profound strategic implications for the Philippines' position in the Indo-Pacific maritime order. It is both a defensive measure and a diplomatic statement – a law designed not only to regulate movement within our waters, but to project order amid regional disorder.

The law is a strategic response to China's expansive activities in the South China Sea and its assertion of the "nine-dash line". By designating sea lanes and restricting military or intelligence activities, the Philippines establishes a legal mechanism to challenge unauthorized foreign presence within its waters. Every time a foreign vessel deviates from an authorized route, lingers unnecessarily, or conducts prohibited operations, the Philippines now has clear statutory authority to respond – not with escalation, but with lawful enforcement. In this way, R.A. 12065 converts law into deterrence, using international legality to counter unilateral actions.

The Act also strengthens the Philippines' role as a rules-based maritime partner in the Indo-Pacific. By aligning our domestic legislation with UNCLOS, we reaffirm our adherence to the rules-based order – a foundation that supports deeper cooperation with allies such as the United States, Australia, Japan, and other ASEAN states. Through this alignment, the Philippines enhances its credibility in joint patrols, defense cooperation, and capacity-building programs. It creates a legal environment conducive to collaborative maritime security, not confrontation.

The Act empowers Philippine enforcement agencies – particularly the Philippine Coast Guard, Navy, and Maritime Industry Authority – by providing legal clarity for action. It serves as the legal foundation for patrolling and monitoring designated lanes, intercepting violators, and securing budgetary support for surveillance systems, radar networks, and vessels. It transforms maritime law into enforcement capability, allowing the Philippines to move from mere assertion to effective control of its archipelagic waters.

Together with the Maritime Zones Act, the Archipelagic Sea Lanes Act operationalizes the 2016

Arbitral Ruling. Where the Arbitral Tribunal affirmed our sovereign rights and maritime entitlements, the Archipelagic Sea Lanes Act enforces them in practice – ensuring that transit through our waters occurs under conditions defined by Philippine law. This coherence between domestic legislation and international ruling strengthens our legal claim and consolidates our international legitimacy.

By codifying clear "rules of the road" for foreign passage, it helps prevent miscalculation and accidental escalation – particularly in heavily transited routes. Yet, the law also acknowledges its own geopolitical weight. While it reaffirms Philippine sovereignty, it may test the resolve of foreign powers accustomed to broader navigational freedoms.

The Philippine Archipelagic Sea Lanes Act embodies the balance of prudence and principle – asserting our rights while preserving the channels of diplomacy. It is both a legal instrument and a strategic compass. It strengthens sovereignty, ensures order, and aligns national policy with international law. It tells the world that the Philippines are not a passive archipelago adrift in regional currents, but an archipelagic state with clear laws, capable enforcement, and strategic foresight. By defining how foreign vessels may pass through our seas, we remind all nations that the Philippines governs its waters – not through confrontation, but through the rule of law and respect for order.

R.A. 12065 is not merely about lanes in the sea. It is about the path toward maritime stability, where sovereignty, security, and responsibility sail together under one flag – the flag of the Republic of the Philippines.

CHAPTER 11

The Struggle Continues

The passing of the Maritime Zones Act and the Archipelagic Sea Lanes Act was of huge importance and lasting significance, but the struggle against China's continuing attempts to impose their view of the world on Filipinos continued. Beijing's response to these two landmark laws – condemning them as illegal and redoubling the pressure on Filipino fishermen and coastguard personnel at sea – demonstrated that legislation alone could not resolve a contest of will between a small nation determined to defend its legal rights and a superpower that had decided to ignore them.

What emerged in the years surrounding the passage of the two Acts was a picture of Chinese activity that was more pervasive and more sophisticated than the use of water cannons and aggressive maneuvers in the West Philippine Sea that had come to define the conflict in the public mind. China was fighting the Philippines on multiple fronts: through Hollywood films; the use of illegal data-recording drones in the waters beneath our oceans; disinformation spread by China-funded "troll farms" appearing in the social media feeds of millions of ordinary Filipinos; and good "old-fashioned" espionage, using spies to gather information about Philippine security bases and military activities.

I chaired hearings that brought each of these threats before the Senate, drawing on the testimony of legal scholars and cybersecurity experts and of Filipinos from all walks of life: fishermen, military officers, diplomats and intelligence officers. The story they told was of a campaign of persistent and malicious interference in Filipino affairs, designed to promote China's political agenda and undermine Philippine interests. But the story was also one of Filipino vigilance and the diligent prosecution of illegal activities.

The *Barbie* Movie (July 2023)

In July 2023, the Hollywood movie studio, Warner Bros., released *Barbie*, a satirical take on the fantasy world represented by the ubiquitous Barbie dolls – and of course, of Barbie's doll-world "boyfriend", Ken. The film was a huge commercial and critical success. But there was a problem – at least for the countries of Southeast Asia.

In one scene, Barbie stands briefly in front of a map of the world. It is, intentionally, like a map of the world drawn from memory by a child. Parts of the map are wildly inaccurate. The United Kingdom, flagged with a crown to denote the country's monarchy, is bigger than the whole of Europe, which is depicted as an island. This, I assume, is intended to humorously reflect the fact that the average American is aware of Great Britain and its monarchy, but is much hazier about the rest of Europe. The Indian Subcontinent seems to have gone missing, unless it is part of a fairly shapeless large island clearly marked 'Asia' – but this landmass seems to feature a rough drawing of the

Great Wall of China and clearly features four small red stars – a key feature of China's flag.

The problem, from a southeast Asian perspective, was that off the coast of "Asia", a wavy dotted line was clearly drawn, suspiciously reminiscent of China's "nine-dash line". It wasn't U-shaped, like China's own imaginary line, but it was the kind of thing a child might draw if it had seen a map of the world featuring the nine-dash line in the South China Sea and tried to incorporate it in their rough drawing. It seemed to give credence, even at a subliminal level, to the validity of the nine-dash line – something that the Permanent Court of Arbitration had ruled to be a legal nonsense.

Vietnam banned *Barbie* from being shown in the country because of this depiction of a rudimentary nine-dash line, having already banned two previous films – Universal Pictures' *Abominable* (2019) and Sony Interactive Entertainment's *Uncharted* (2022) – both of which had briefly featured real maps showing the nine-dash line. I believed that we should also ban the movie, or at least challenge the appropriate body to make a ruling – in this case the Movie and Television Review and Classification Board (MTRCB). On July 4, 2023, I appeared on *CNN Philippines* on "The Final Word with Rico Hizon" program, to argue that banning the movie "would be a form of symbolic solidarity with other Asian, neighboring countries (…) like Vietnam." I said also that I thought the release of the movie "will not just be injurious to the prestige of the Republic of the Philippines, but would be contrary to what our country fought for and achieved under the arbitration ruling of 2016." By that time, I had already petitioned the MTRCB asking them to block the film's release in the Philippines because of its depiction of China's nine-dash line – in however "cartoonish" a form.

The MTRCB conducted two reviews of the film and consulted with both the Philippine Department of Foreign Affairs (DFA) and the Office of the Solicitor General. In their conclusion, the MTRCB argued, correctly, that the map in question was a "childlike crayon drawing," and that dotted line shown was not U-shaped, featured only eight dashes, and that the Philippines, Malaysia, and Indonesia were not visible. This was true, but seemed to miss the point that any kind of "dashed line" shown off the coast of "Asia" was provocative, and risked giving credence to China's debunked claims.

The MTRCB ultimately decided to allow the film to be shown but asked Warner Bros. to blur the lines and warned producers and distributors that any future films that featured the nine-dash line would be banned. It was clear that the MTRCB had taken my point seriously. Even though it judged that the *Barbie* movie could be released, with the offending lines blurred, it was agreeing that any depiction of the nine-dash line in movies should be prohibited in future.

Although the argument about the depiction of the nine-dash line in a satirical film about the secret life of dolls might seem trivial and not worth challenging, the effects of China's relentless attempt to persuade the world of the reality of its fictitious line in the sea must not be underestimated.

Talking to *The Philippine Daily Inquirer* in the wake of the incident, Dr. Chester Cabalza, president and founder of the International Development and Security Cooperation, the Manila-based policy research think tank, reminded us of the power of popular culture to affect our thinking. "(F)ilms and arts are persuasive platforms in the cognition of our understanding on changing narratives and geopolitics," he told the newspaper. "Sometimes most moviegoers are not critical of the facts and they easily believe in fictional images and dialogues in movies."[100]

Internally, of course, China has an iron grip on the narrative: every schoolchild in China is taught in an environment that presents the nine-dash line as simple historical and geographic fact. The line must appear on every map. It features on every Chinese passport – which is why, for a time, Vietnam refused to stamp Chinese passports showing the line. In China, Google Maps has been forced to show the nine-dash line.

Dr Bill Hayton, associate fellow with the Asia-Pacific programme at Chatham House, talked about how far-reaching China's propaganda efforts are. "In my book, *The Invention of China*," said Hayton, "I talk about China's maritime claim and about maps and how various companies got into trouble for not printing the line on their map. I once met someone who worked for a Chinese conservation organization and their projects were in the middle of China, nowhere near the coast. When they published their annual reports, the map they used had to show the whole of China with the nine-dash shaped line."[101]

Thomas Shattuck is a Senior Program Manager at the University of Pennsylvania's Perry World House and an expert on the US role in the Indo Pacific. He argues that US film makers have been too willing to follow China's line in the hope of gaining or retaining access to the lucrative China market. Talking about the *Barbie* movie incident,

Shattuck said, "I was surprised that they did that in the *Barbie* movie because I thought we were past that era of 'if we do this one thing to make China happy, they'll let us screen the movie and get the PRC [People's Republic of China] market'. We've seen airlines do it by agreeing to use 'Taiwan, China' instead of 'Taiwan' because China would say, 'If you don't do that, then you can't fly into our country.' The clothing retailer Gap had a map on a T shirt of mainland China without the nine-dash line, and they made them change that. So there's a long history of this kind of bullying."

The lesson is clear. China takes its nine-dash line propaganda extremely seriously. And the purpose of the propaganda is to persuade the world to accept something that is not true and has been shown to be untrue in an international court of law: that China's imaginary line in the South China Sea has any kind of validity or legal force. It is a self-interested lie that must be called out as such every time China reiterates it – in any form, including apparently innocent split-second frames in popular movies.

The HY-119 Submersible Drone

On December 30, 2024 – three weeks after President Marcos had signed the Maritime Zones Act and the Archipelagic Sea Lanes Act into law – three fishermen from the small island of Iniwaran, off the coast of San Pascual in Masbate province, were on their way to market with a catch of fish when they spotted something unusual in the water. Fisherman Rodney Valenzuela, who was steering the bangka that morning, described what he saw when he testified before my Senate committee on January 15, 2025. "On December 30 at six in the morning, we were taking our fish to the town of San Pascual. We passed what I thought was just a buoy, which fishermen use as a marker. When we got close, I saw that it was larger than that, so I turned back. And when we brought it up, my companion said, 'It's a bomb!'"

(Author is shown with a captured submersible drone during a Senate hearing)

What Valenzuela and his companions had hauled out of Masbate Strait was not a bomb, but a twelve-foot underwater drone. The markings "HY-119" were clearly visible on its casing – the HY-119 sea drone is manufactured by a company based in Tianjin, China. It had an antenna protruding perhaps three feet above the waterline. These underwater gliders have no form of propulsion and are designed to ride ocean currents while gathering hydrographic data which might have commercial, scientific, or military value, using an onboard battery to transmit the data back to base – wherever that might be – via its antenna, whenever the drone was on the surface.

The fishermen, uncertain what to make of the device, had brought it to shore, left it in the boat, gone to sell their fish, and only later reported it to barangay officials, who contacted the police. Four officers were needed to carry the device from the dockside to the police station, where it sat on a table for some time. An Explosive Ordnance Disposal team drove from Legazpi, two provinces away, arriving at 11 p.m. – nine hours after the initial report. They wrapped the antenna in aluminum foil to block any tracking signal and finally declared the device safe. It was then transferred to the Philippine Navy for forensic examination.

The Special Committee on Philippine Maritime and Admiralty Zones met on January 15, 2025, to discuss the issue, with me as Chairperson. Committee members and resource persons included representatives from the Office of the Undersecretary of Migration Affairs, the Department of Foreign Affairs (DFA), the Department of Justic (DOJ), the Department of National Defense (DND), the National Security Council (NSC), the Philippine National Police (PNP), and the Philippine Navy and Coast Guard.

I opened the hearing by setting out the questions that needed answering: "As everyone knows, our Philippine Maritime Zones Law and the Archipelagic Sea Lanes Law were just signed on December 8. Was this drone included in any of the categories of vessels contained in the new laws I mentioned?" I asked if the drone might be sovereign property that should be returned to its owners? Was it a warship that should be given sovereign recognition? Should it be considered as a civilian vessel? Could it be an autonomous vessel that was part of research being conducted by a mother ship? Was this drone part of foreign interference in our oceans, involved in reconnaissance and espionage? Did drones like this require a change in our laws? Should there be a warning to our fishermen that if they see something similar, they should not catch it with their nets but should report it to the Philippine Coast Guard and Philippine Navy? Was it armed, either for attack or for self-destruction? Was it simply part of the daily activities in the ocean that we could just ignore?

Or perhaps, I added, this drone was only one of many other drones that we were unaware of, operating silently in the waters beneath our shipping lanes and fishing grounds, that might turn out to be a greater threat than we had realized.

The representative from the PNP Maritime Group, Jonathan Cabal, told the hearing that their research confirmed that the device was a Chinese-made submersible drone which he took to be of "military grade or for scientific purposes". Testimony from the DND's Undersecretary, Ignacio Madriaga, revealed that this was not the first such discovery. Previous drones of a similar specification had been recovered in Philippine waters – a total of five, including the recently discovered device – but that the PNP had not been able to make any definitive conclusion about the devices' origin or ownership since no one, as in the present case, had yet come forward to claim them.

The legal classification of the drone was significant but hard to determine. Was it a warship or a civilian vessel – in which case, under the newly-passed Archipelagic Sea Lanes Act, it would need to follow designated routes? A weapon – in which case the Geneva convention on weapons might apply?

Ignacio Madriaga, from the Office of the Undersecretary for Strategic Assessment and Planning, at the DND told the committee that the drone's purpose was to collect data. It was capable of mapping the subsurface and collecting data on hydrography, including water salinity, temperature and depth – data that was important for submarine navigation. "As far as the defense department is concerned," Madriaga said, "we are treating it as a national security matter, whether it is unarmed or uncrewed", saying that the department considered it as "a violation of our territory."

I noted that whoever was receiving his data, be it for commercial, scientific or military reasons, it was not the Philippines. The data that the device was transmitting would have been received by "the human in the loop," and that human was not a Filipino. Some other nation was gathering information about our waters, "and they are the ones who will benefit from it, not us."

Madriaga also explained how the unpowered submersible drone could be released and allowed to follow known sea currents to explore the waters of our archipelago. He drew an analogy with the high-altitude spy ballon that had drifted over Canada and the US in 2023, carried by the jet stream, passing over many sensitive sites before being shot down over the Atlantic by the US Air Force. That balloon was known to have come from China, and Madriaga was at pains to say that he was not saying that "the same country" was involved in the case of the submersible drone. The marking on the submersible – HY-119 – showed that it was a Haiyi or "Sea Wing" glider, made in Tianjin, China but, nevertheless, it would be necessary to confirm that the device had been deliberately dispatched by China itself before a diplomatic protest could be lodged.

Speaking for the DOJ, Senior State Counsel Fretti Ganchoon confirmed that if the drone was conducting scientific research in any of the Philippine Maritime Zones or internal waters this would require express consent under Article 245 of UNCLOS. Ganchoon also confirmed that under the Maritime Zones Act and Archipelagic Sea Lanes Act, the presence of the drone in Philippine waters was "most likely a violation of either of our sovereign rights or our sovereignty."

The hearing spent some time discussing the Philippine's ability to counter submarine threats. Ganchoon stressed that the Philippines land area is only about 30,000 square kilometers while our maritime area is two million square kilometers, which meant that there was an urgent need for what she called maritime domain awareness, which should include the subsurface of our waters. "We should know what is happening underwater, Mr. Chair," said Ganchoon. "So, we need to upgrade, and we need to prioritize our capability for maritime domain awareness, especially maritime domain underwater awareness."

By the time of the April hearings, the drone inquiry had expanded into something much wider-ranging and even more disturbing. On April 23 and 24, 2025, I chaired other meetings of the special committee. The National Bureau of Investigation (NBI), the National Intelligence Coordinating Agency (NICA), the NSC, the Armed Forces, the Navy and the Coast Guard presented evidence of a systematic espionage campaign operating across the Philippines.

NBI Senior Agent Alvin Bernardo described three separate arrest operations. The first, which became known as the "Makati 1" case, took place on January 17, 2025. Deng Yuanqing, a Chinese national and a graduate of People's Liberation Army University of Science and Technology in Nanjing, China, who was married to a Filipino woman and was a permanent residence visa holder, had been arrested in the San Antonio area of Makati along with two Filipino accomplices. It was discovered that their vehicle, a Toyota RAV4, had been fitted with LIDAR (light detection and ranging) and GNSS-RTK satellite positioning equipment capable of topographic mapping to centimeter-level accuracy. It had been moving around critical infrastructure sites since December 2024. "Everything this vehicle can pass through," Bernado told the hearing, "they can conduct topographic mapping. And what (they)'re doing here, is they're going to our critical infrastructures like military camps, ports, seaports, communications towers, power grids."

I asked where the data was being sent. "According to our investigation," said Bernardo, "the data and information he obtained was accessed by an IP address that is located in China."

The second operation, known as "the Palawan 5'," involved five Chinese nationals who had installed a solar-powered, remotely accessible high-definition camera in a treehouse at a Palawan resort, trained on the open sea to record the movements of Philippine naval vessels. The third operation took place in Subic, where six Chinese nationals and one Filipino were arrested for maritime spying near the naval base while posing as fishermen. Again, attorney Van Homer Angkuben, an Executive Officer for the NBI's Cybercrime Division, confirmed that it was believed that the data being collected was being transmitted to China.

When I asked NBI Senior Agent Bernardo if there was any indication this was part of a wider espionage network, his reply was unequivocal: "We believe so, Mr. Chair. This is just the tip of the iceberg."

"If it's the tip of the iceberg," I said, "it means, if you caught five, there are still hundreds out there." "It's possible, Mr. Chair," replied Angkuben on behalf of the NBI.

On April 29, 2025 – just six days after the April 23 hearing – the NBI made another arrest that brought the espionage campaign to the heart of the capital, on the eve of our national elections.

An informant had tipped off the NBI that someone had been seen loading a machine into a vehicle – a machine that resembled the LIDAR mapping equipment seized in the earlier Makati arrest. NBI agents began car-tailing the vehicle on April 24. They nearly lost the first operative: he left the Philippines on Saturday, April 26, leaving his Makati apartment and departing the country – perhaps aware he was being watched, or perhaps following a pre-arranged rotation schedule. It would emerge later that his replacement, a Chinese national named Tak Hoi Lao, did not know the identity of the operative he was replacing – a classic piece of espionage tradecraft, "compartmentalizing" each agent from the other. Tak rented a new apartment in Makati and resumed the pervious agent's operations, driving the vehicle containing the machine around central Manila.

The NBI's Technical Intelligence Division tracked the vehicle as it moved through Metro Manila over the following days. The route it drove was not random. It passed the Supreme Court and the Department of Justice. It circled Villamor Air Base, the headquarters of the Philippine Air Force. It drove along Intramuros, past the Bureau of Internal Revenue. Three or four times, it came back to the same block in Intramuros and drove slowly past the offices of the Commission on Elections (COMELEC) at Palacio del Gobernador. The midterm elections were only thirteen days away.

The machine the vehicle was carrying was not a was not LIDAR surveying equipment, it was an International Mobile Subscriber's Identity (IMSI) catcher, capable of mimicking a legitimate mobile cell tower. Phones in the vicinity inadvertently connect to the IMSI, which then quietly harvests the unique identities and metadata of every mobile within range: numbers dialed, caller IDs and duration of call. The device had an effective radius of between five hundred meters and three kilometers; in a dense urban area like Intramuros, with its many offices and government buildings and tens of thousands of pedestrians, that range swept up an enormous number of devices. By the time NBI agents moved to intercept the vehicle at 1:30 p.m. on April 29, near the COMELEC offices, the Technical Intelligence Division confirmed that the machine had already accessed approximately five thousand mobile subscriber identities. An IMSI device is also capable of sending messages which appear to the recipient of the call to have come from the "captured" phone number, tricking people into thinking they have received a call or message from someone they perhaps know.

Tak Hoi Lao was arrested. He was brought before the Department of Justice the following day and held at a secure NBI facility at the Bureau of Corrections in Muntinlupa. The machine was secured as evidence.

I brought NBI Director Ferdinand Lavin before my committee on May 5, 2025 – one week before election day – to present the details of the arrest. I was struck by something he noted almost in passing: the NBI still required a court warrant to examine the computer data on the seized machine. They had already applied and they were fast-tracking the application, said Lavin, but the process would take time.

I put it plainly: "At this point in time, we are not certain whether the data has been transmitted elsewhere, whether the data has been used, whether the data has been manipulated." Five thousand phone identities, harvested within range of the national election commission, by a Chinese operative driving a circuit past the Supreme Court and the Air Force headquarters. And the forensic examination – which might reveal what those identities had been used for – could not begin without a warrant. By the time the NBI was able to complete their forensics, the election might already be over. I also asked about the subject of the earlier arrest, Deng Yuanqing, and asked if there was any connection between him and the new arrests and whether it had been confirmed that he was a member of the People's Liberation Army. I was told that investigations were still proceeding. It did feel as if we were only seeing the "tip of the iceberg."

COMELEC Chairman George Garcia was at pains to reassure the hearing – and the public – that no election data had been compromised. The counting machines, all 110,000 of them, were standalone devices not connected to any network. The actual election results, before transmission, were printed and physically posted outside each precinct, so any attempt to alter the transmitted data could be checked against the paper originals. But he acknowledged that the NBI's evidence made it impossible to deny the commission was being targeted. There was also evidence of a disinformation campaign on social media targeting the elections. Garcia confirmed that the NBI had noticed that a post saying, for example, that the election would be rigged – attempting to throw doubt on the integrity of the elections – would receive 700,000 views within 30 minutes and 32,000 comments would immediately be posted in response – an entirely unnatural pattern that strongly suggested a campaign of automated amplification. Other posts had suggested that voters would need to present National ID to vote – which was, of course, untrue. Another said that the elections would be held, not on May 12, but on May 10, because of the extremely hot weather. COMELEC was able to put out rebuttals of all these attempts to confuse and mislead voters, but Garcia said that he was grateful for the current investigation because it confirmed "what we have been saying for a long time" – the existence of disinformation campaigns designed to interfere with Philippine elections and affect their outcome.

I cited a confidential report from the cyber-disinformation specialists, Cyabra, which had found that 45% of online conversations surrounding the 2025 Philippine midterm elections were being driven by fake accounts, bots, and sock puppet profiles – an astonishingly high figure, given that the global average for disinformation in sensitive elections was 7-10% percent. Even Romania's contested 2024 election – widely cited as a case of severe Russian interference – had recorded 'only' 16% fake engagement. The Philippine elections were being attacked by a disinformation campaign of unprecedented scale and ferocity.

The InfinitUS Troll Farm

Some two weeks earlier, on the morning of April 24, 2025, I had presented to the hearing a folder of documents that would prove, in my view, the most disturbing evidence yet of the scope of China's operations against the Philippines.

I had obtained a copy of a service agreement. The client was identified as: "The People's Republic of China, represented by its Director of the Media and Public Relations, Chinese Embassy, Mr. Wu Chenqi." The provider was "Infinitus Marketing Solutions, Inc.," a Makati-based corporation registered with the Philippine Securities and Exchange Commission, with two Chinese nationals, Min Li and Pin Li, listed as cofounders in the company's incorporation documents, alongside Filipino nationals, in compliance with the Philippine's rule that media companies, and some other regulated sectors, must have at least 60% ownership by Filipinos. The contract specified a bank transfer to a UnionBank account. The Bank of China cheque I then displayed to the committee showed a payment of ₱930,000 – part of a contract with a total value of approximately ₱3.7 million, or around US$63,000.

I had also obtained copies of monthly reports that InfinitUS supplied to the Chinese Embassy to document its work on their behalf. The reports revealed that InfinitUS managed what the documents themselves described as an "army" of 330 social media accounts: 300 on Facebook and 30 on X (previously known as Twitter). Eleven operatives ran the accounts, each maintaining over twenty fake personas. The personas were crafted to appear as ordinary Filipinos: teachers, students, business professionals, members of the Armed Forces. Instruction documents specified that operatives should use legitimate mobile phone numbers rather than email addresses to bypass platform verification; they would steal real profile photographs and distort them with filters to evade AI detection tools. The reports boasted that these fake accounts had created over 50,000 Filipino friends and followers – drawing genuine citizens into conversations and comment threads with fabricated personas, talking about topics chosen by Beijing and promoting Beijing's agenda.

To take one example close to my own efforts, four days after President Marcos signed the Maritime Zones Act into law on November 8, 2024, the trolls were deployed to respond with negative messages: "*China has all the right to oppose this because it runs counter to their territorial stand. These new maritime laws and protocols will just worsen our conflict with China.*" "*The Philippine government should not have passed this law because they very well know that it will only intensify our conflict with China and other Asian neighbors.*" "*China will not be the only country to be affected by the new maritime laws, our other Asian neighbors who also have territorial disputes, claims in the South China Sea, will be affected.*" The messages were clearly generating the hoped-for response. Somebody replied to one of the troll farm's messages, saying, "*Unbelievable. That was my reaction when I first read about these new maritime claims by our country. Why would our government do acts that would further escalate our tensions with China?*"

One of the "army's" tasks was to persuade Filipinos that China was essential to their economy and prosperity. Without China, fake messages said, Filipinos would be "dirt poor people in a backwater country full of mud."

The troll farm had been used to spread other strategic, political or military-related messages favoring China. A special video was produced and disseminated criticizing the deployment of US Typhoon missiles in the Philippines; there were attacks on the Marcos political dynasty and the promotion of a controversial US article suggesting the world's leading auto manufacturers needed to partner with China's automakers because of the latter's dominant stature. The Facebook account of Representative Robert Barbers of Surigao, a vocal advocate for Philippine maritime legislation, was flooded with negative responses to his statements about China's stance on the South China Sea.

The NSC's Assistant Director General, Jonathan Malaya, confirmed what the documents revealed. "What we are seeing, is that there are many narratives emerging from Beijing that are being amplified by third-party individuals, who are their proxies." These narratives were often timed to coincide with sensitive political moments: the Balikatan (shoulder-to-shoulder) joint military exercises between the Philippines and the US, for example, would be decried by the troll farm as a threat to regional peace and stability. Malaya also confirmed that I had been the target of attacks by the Filipino troll army during the passage of the Maritime Zones Act and the Archipelagic Sea Lanes Act. I allowed myself a wry smile at this point in the hearing: "So that's why I get bashed every day," I said. "It's been a long time."

Francisco Acedillo, Deputy Director of Cyber and Emerging Threats at NICA, highlighted the significance of China's 2015 Military Strategy, which he said marked a critical evolution in China's military doctrine. The very first element of this new strategy was information dominance: "prioritizing control of the information space as a prerequisite for military success." Acedillo described what he saw as the four most significant practical implications of this for the Philippines. "One is the development of sophisticated cyber capabilities that could target Philippine government, military, and critical infrastructure," Acedillo told the hearing. "Second are enhanced electronic warfare capabilities for potential deployment in disputed areas like the South China Sea; third is investment in advanced surveillance systems to monitor military activities and communications; and fourth, the creation of information operations capabilities to influence public opinion and political discourse."

I asked him to repeat the last sentence – “the creation of information operations capabilities to influence public opinion and political discourse” – to underscore its significance. I asked if NSC or NICA had seen evidence of foreign interference in the 2025 elections, particularly targeting candidates with strong pro-sovereignty or anti-China positions. The NSC’s Deputy Director general, Jonathan Malaya answered: “There are indications, Mr. Chairman, that information operations are being conducted that are Chinese state sponsored in the Philippines and are actually interfering in the forthcoming elections.”

“So does this mean that China has ongoing operations to support the candidates they want to win, and to oppose the candidates they don't want to win?” I asked directly.

“Yes, there are indications of that, Mr. Chairman,” Malaya replied.

Addressing the committee, I pointed out the sinister truth behind the documents we had obtained: “We have a Chinese government paying, via its embassy in Manila, Philippine nationals working for a troll farm to attack our country, to attack the administration, using fake names and with clear guidance to keep secret whom they are actually working for. (…) (T)hey recruit and pay or coerce our own citizens, in this case, to attack our country's policies – what the Navy does, what the Coast Guard does, what the Armed Forces do – behind a fake social media account, trying to manipulate the Philippine public.”

InfinitUS subsequently denied the allegations raised in the hearing – that it was running a “troll farm” of fake social media accounts spreading misinformation on China’ s behalf – calling the service agreement I had revealed “unauthenticated, unsigned, and completely unfamiliar to our company” – “at best, a forgery crafted to fit a political narrative.” The company confirmed that the cheque was real, describing the payment as “legal and justified” for services to “diplomatic institutions,” and threatened legal action over what it called the “unauthorized public exposure” of its financial records. Its website and Facebook page went offline in the days following the hearing.

CHAPTER 12

Enough is Enough

On May 5, 2025, eleven days after the April 24 hearing – and eleven days after InfinitUS had publicly called its service agreement with the Chinese Embassy "a forgery crafted to fit a political narrative" – the company's CEO, Paul Li, appeared before my committee under oath. His real name was Pin Li; a Chinese national who had lived in the Philippines for more than twenty years. As we saw in the previous chapter, Pin Li was one of the cofounders of the company that he ran. He had chosen to come back from abroad for the hearing, he said, even though his Filipino wife was undergoing treatment in China for Stage 4 cancer. He said he wanted to face the allegations with candor. "I come not to hide, not to delay," he told the committee, "but to face this proceeding with full respect for this Committee." He categorically denied any involvement in the troll farm. The service agreement, he said, was not known to him and had never been authorized by the company. When we showed him a copy of the contract, signed by the company's marketing director, Myka Poynton, he said, "That is not her wet signature. It is just e-signature. We do not know how it got there."

We then showed the Bank of China cheque. I had already established at the April 24 hearing that a cheque payable to InfinitUS for ₱930,000 had been issued from the Bank of China. Li confirmed under oath that the cheque was real, that his company had received it, and that it was payment for a follow-up balance arising from an event held at Manila Hotel on June 8, 2023: the "Award for Promoting Philippines-China Understanding," which President Marcos and members of Cabinet had attended. The additional costs, he explained, arose because of last-minute COVID-19 requirements – antigen testing kits, face masks, and face shields had been requested by the President's security office.

But by June 2023, the World Health Organization had declared the COVID-19 pandemic over. Schools were open, airlines were operating without restrictions, and the Philippines had long since abandoned face masks and antigen tests. I told him that the committee would not accept documents citing COVID requirements for a June 2023 event. He had either confused his narrative, or he was lying. Then I showed him the document he had produced as a supporting invoice: it was dated September 5, 2023 – three months after the supposed June event – and it was a budget proposal, not an invoice.

Next, I showed him a Chinese-language scope of work document bearing the InfinitUS logo. The committee had commissioned a translation. The heading read: "Project: Publicity Guidance Team of the Chinese Embassy in the Philippines." The instructions specified conducting public opinion guidance on Twitter and Facebook, maintaining real-time communication with a crisis response team at the embassy, and providing monthly reports on implementation. The total contract value: ₱930,000 – precisely matching the cheque Li had just confirmed was genuine. He said it was the first time he had seen the document.

I then showed him the monthly engagement reports submitted to the Chinese Embassy – the "Important Highlights of the Month" that detailed how what it described as the "army" of troll accounts had performed. Li said he had never seen the reports. He said he had never seen the objectives document. He said he was not familiar with the scope of work. Each document carried the InfinitUS logo and referenced the same ₱930,000 figure.

Finally, I produced copies of immigration records. Li had suggested to the hearing that he had not travelled much to China since coming to the Philippines 20 years ago. He and his wife had travelled to China in 2009 to get married there, but since then he had travelled there again only recently, because his wife was receiving treatment there for her cancer. I told Li that I had flight details – airlines, dates, and gate numbers – showing that he, his marketing director Myka Poynton, and Filipino cofounder Ruby Gestiada had all made multiple trips to China across the preceding years. Gestiada had gone to Canton in December 2024 and again in January 2025. Poynton had visited Beijing, Shanghai and Dayong multiple times through 2024. The records showed flight details for Li himself going back to 2019, with trips to Xiamen, Hong Kong, Shanghai, Canton and Beijing. Li attributed the trips to medical visits for his wife. I noted that the records predated her illness by years.

In the end, I lost patience with Li's evasions. "I cannot tolerate any more lies," I said to him. "especially at this period when we are confronted not just with lies but disinformation. You are making this Committee part of the disinformation campaign."

I concluded: "I think this Committee has done more than enough to tie the dots: from the arrested spies of the Palawan, referring to the Palawan 5; to the El Grande spies; to the Makati spies; to the Intramuros spies, more than nineteen and still growing; to the submersible drones; to the disinformation campaign, which is still ongoing and still growing. The Committee is confident that we will come up with more robust legislative measures that will confront all of this. Commonwealth Act 616 is not enough. The current cyber security laws would not suffice. We still need a more dynamic and proactive legislative framework, but we need the cooperation of all." (Commonwealth Act 616 is the Philippines' 1941 anti-espionage law, long predating the digital age.)

There was one moment of unintended comedy in an otherwise grim proceeding. I had been questioning NBI Director Lavin about the IMSI catcher arrest earlier in the hearing and paused to ask him to clarify for the public what "IMSI" actually stood for. He explained: International Mobile Subscriber's Identity. I then observed, with a straight face, that IMSI was also the corporate acronym for InfinitUS Marketing Solutions, Inc. "Just a coincidence, right?" I asked. The NBI broke into barely suppressed laughter. I instructed the stenographers not to record it.

At the end of the hearing, I said I believed that if we did not get a grip on this kind of espionage, we would lose our very sovereignty. "We have to bear in mind that cyber sovereignty is our right to govern our digital space. I believe that this issue is not over. There are many more like Infinitus out there that we have not yet identified. There are many more drones now under our oceans that have not yet been caught. There are many more IMSI grabbers roaming around us."

The final element of the picture that emerged from these episodes was in some ways the most disturbing of all, because it involved not the activities of Chinese state agents in the Philippines, but the detention of Filipino citizens in China – students who had gone to Hainan on a provincial scholarship programme and found themselves caught in the crossfire of a diplomatic confrontation.

The arrests of Chinese nationals in the Philippines had proceeded steadily through the first months of 2025. Two days after those arrests, the Chinese Embassy in Manila issued a travel advisory warning Chinese citizens about what they described as "frequent harassment" of Chinese nationals by Philippine law enforcement. Then, on April 3, 2025, China announced that three Filipinos had been arrested in China for alleged espionage.

The three were David Servañez, Albert Endencia, and Nathalie Plizardo. All three were former recipients of the Hainan Government Scholarship Program, established under a 2017 sisterhood agreement between Hainan Province and Palawan Province that had sent fifty Palawan students to study at Hainan Normal University between 2018 and 2022. The three had graduated in 2022, returned to the Philippines, and subsequently gone back to China after receiving job offers in Hainan. Their families had lost contact with them between October 2024 and January 2025. Palawan provincial authorities had known of their detention since at least November 2024 but had maintained confidentiality to protect the families. The arrests had clearly predated our espionage investigations in the

Philippines and were being brought to our attention now as a threat.

China's Foreign Ministry spokesman Guo Jiakun said the Philippines had "concocted a series of so-called Chinese spy cases." Chinese state media described the three Filipinos as long-term residents and accused them of having loitered near military facilities, gathering classified information on Chinese military deployments. The National Security Council's ADG Jonathan Malaya rejected this narrative. The three, he noted, were "ordinary Filipino citizens with no military training" and no criminal records, who had been "vetted and screened by the Chinese government prior to their arrival there." Most tellingly, the "confessions" that had appeared in Chinese state media referenced institutions that did not exist – a "Philippine Intelligence Agency" or "Philippine Spy Intelligence Services," agencies that have never existed in the Philippine government. The statements, Malaya observed, had clearly been scripted.

The Philippines requested access to the students under the 2009 Philippines-China Consular Agreement, ratified in 2012, which required China to notify the Philippines within four days of a Filipino's detention and permit consular visits. China's response to these requests was, at the time of the April hearings, still awaited.

By April 2025, I had filed Senate Bill 2951, the Counter Foreign Interference Activity or Anti-Spying Law, creating penalties for foreign interference in the Philippines through hostile intelligence activity. I called for the establishment of a foreign influence task force to coordinate the agencies that had, across the preceding months, been uncovering the same campaign from different angles. I called for the update of the Philippines' espionage law, then over eighty years old – a statute designed for a world in which spying meant men with cameras rather than autonomous underwater drones and AI-assisted troll networks.

These legislative proposals were the direct consequence of what the hearings had revealed: a campaign that was comprehensive, coordinated, and ongoing. The Maritime Zones Act and the Archipelagic Sea Lanes Act had established, in domestic law, exactly what the Philippines' rights were. But a law, however carefully drafted, requires an enforcement infrastructure equal to the threats it confronts. The drones, the troll farms, the spy networks, and the detained scholars were China's answer to Filipino legislation – an answer delivered not through diplomacy or legal argument, but through the full spectrum of gray-zone pressure available to a state determined not to accept the judgment of international law.

In my closing statement on April 24, 2025 – after two days of testimony spanning drones, spy networks and troll farms – I had addressed the significance of these events, which I felt represented a direct attack on our sovereignty.

I would like to paraphrase that closing speech here, in what I think is a fitting close to this chapter.

So we've been dragged around here. We have a Chinese government, via its embassy in Manila, paying Philippine nationals working for a troll farm to attack our country. To attack the administration using fake names, with clear guidance to keep who they are actually working for secret. They recruit and pay or coerce our own citizens to attack our country's policies – what the Navy does, what the Coast Guard does, what the Armed Forces do – trying to manipulate the Philippine public. These fake social media accounts have criticized the president, criticized Cabinet officials, criticized outspoken legislators, criticized the Philippine government.

For what did they criticize them? For having the nerve to stand up in defense of the West Philippine Sea; for having the nerve not to allow our own seas to be taken by force. What is happening is outrageous behavior; it is a violation of every international norm. It is certainly not the way that friends treat friends, and it makes a mockery of the Chinese Embassy's talk of friendship.

We should not turn a blind eye and set aside our findings. Even if China denies it, what we saw yesterday and today were not isolated events. We can be sure that China is not done with their surveillance of our country. The question is: Why do they instruct their trolls to criticize the Philippines' effort to defend itself? The answer is simple and obvious: China does not want the Philippines to have the means to defend its territory and sovereignty. They pretend to be motivated by concerns about peace in the region. At the same time, they undertake a massive campaign of targeted espionage against the Philippines – a multi-pronged effort to gain information and manipulate and ultimately destroy the Philippines' ability to oppose China.

This activity is still ongoing. It is happening everywhere; it is happening here in Metro Manila; it is happening in the provinces; it is happening in the water; it is happening on land; it is happening in Subic Bay; it is happening off the coast of Palawan; it is happening in the West Philippine Sea. We cannot close our ears and eyes and pretend that this will be okay – that this will disappear and that no real damage has been done. We understand why the spies are doing what they are doing, and that is to maximize their ability to harm us.

This attempt at surveillance is an attack on every Filipino. It is an attack on the institutions of our state. It is an attack on our freedom. It is an attack on the ability of every citizen to enjoy free press, learn the truth, speak and be heard, and stand up for ourselves and stand united at this stage in our history. It is an attack on our brave men and women in uniform. Make no mistake, the information that these spies have collected, puts our sons and daughters, our brothers and sisters, directly in harm's way. How can our Navy, our Coast Guard protect themselves or protect us when the Chinese exactly know where they are – where they are going and what exact time they would arrive? Most importantly, it is an attack on our future. It is nothing less than a concerted effort to ensure that China has the intelligence it needs to force us to submit; to accept what they see fit to offer us. It is to conquer us without fighting.

The Chinese have attempted to say through their representative that this is not happening. They have attempted to say that these things are no big deal, and if the Philippines knew what was good for it, they should stop making a fuss. You have seen today the evidence and yesterday, that it is happening. You have seen the evidence that these acts of espionage are connected and they are happening at Beijing's explicit behest. You know, I have been receiving emails saying that this hearing should not continue. But we will not sit idly and behave because Beijing tells us to do so.

Thanks again, I repeat, to the brave men and women of our security forces who have discovered all of this. Also to our fishermen, thank you very much for gathering sensitive information and watching the movements in our territory. We are experiencing this outrageous and disrespectful treatment at the hands of our Chinese neighbors who routinely stress that we are friends, who desire respectful relations. Why are they doing this? They are doing this because as Filipinos, we have the temerity to stand up and say: "What you are doing is wrong, and we will not accept it." We will do what Filipinos have always done when faced with the arrogance of an aggressor's power – we will resist.

I know that you are with me in this Committee when I say, "enough is enough." We can resist by taking immediate steps, like the law that we have filed, Senate Bill 2591, which would punish foreign interference in our country by means of hostile intelligence activity. We can resist by creating a foreign influence task force to root out and stop efforts like this. We can resist by updating our Espionage Law, which is now more than 80 years old. Creating a strong and effective law on spying will ensure that those found to have conducted these harmful activities against our country will be held accountable. We call upon China to immediately halt its hostile and illegal espionage efforts against the Philippines, and we ask the executive branch to take all measures necessary to protect the country from China's continuing depredations. By resisting in these ways, we will be showing China and the world that the Philippines are not quietly submitting to China's coercion and abuse. We are instead raising our voices in unison to defend the fundamental dignity of our people. We are raising our arms in defiance to those who seek to deny our dignity, to claim our lands and seas, and to rob us of our future. Ipaglaban po natin ang Pilipinas. *Let's fight for the Philippines.*

I am grateful to all the agencies here. I hope our work will not end with this hearing. We will continue to fight for our sovereignty. Thank you to the Philippine Navy. Thank you to the Coast Guard. Thank you to the National Security Council. To the men and women in uniform, including the Philippine National Police Maritime Group, to the NICA, to the other government agencies, including the NBI, thank you. Let us continue to confront this crisis. And I am sure we will win.

Close to the time of writing, in March 2026, three men were arrested in Manila for alleged espionage: a suspected Chinese spy and two Filipino accomplices. The men had been trying to collect information about members of the Armed Forces of the Philippines deployed at the *Sierra Madre* vessel at Ayungin Shoal and elsewhere in the West Philippine Sea. The NSC said the arrest had revealed "a serious national security matter", with Filipinos being recruited by China to carry our espionage operations in the Philippines. The NSC confirmed the existence of an "Insider Threat Program" involving several government agencies, designed to counter the growing risk.[102]

The need for ongoing vigilance is clear.

CHAPTER 13

The Enduring Power of Law

The enactment of the Philippine Maritime Zones Act and the Philippine Archipelagic Sea Lanes Act – Republic Acts 12064 and 12065 – represents not only a legal milestone but a strategic turning point in how the Philippines governs, protects, and projects its maritime sovereignty.

These two laws together translate the 2016 Permanent Court of Arbitration (PCA) ruling into a robust domestic framework – one that not only asserts rights but also empowers enforcement, resource management, and diplomacy. Their implications extend well beyond the realm of law. They directly affect the livelihoods of Filipino fishermen, the health of the country's marine ecosystems, the future of its energy security, and the stability of the region.

Let us look at these implications across four critical dimensions.

First, the protection of Philippine fisheries – the lifeblood of many coastal communities, and one of the most tangible benefits of the country's maritime entitlements.

Under RA 12064, the Philippines' Exclusive Economic Zone (EEZ) is now not merely a geographic concept, but a legally enforceable maritime space. It declares the Philippines' sovereign rights to explore, exploit, conserve and manage living resources within 200 nautical miles from its baselines. This legal certainty gives full effect to the Philippine Fisheries Code (RA 8550) and strengthens the nation's ability to act decisively against illegal, unreported, and unregulated (IUU) fishing – particularly by foreign vessels operating within the Philippine's EEZ. It allows the Philippine Coast Guard (PCG), the Bureau of Fisheries and Aquatic Resources (BFAR), and the Navy to confront these violations not merely as administrative infractions but as breaches of national law and sovereignty. But the greater purpose here is not punitive – it is protective. By reinforcing the legal exclusivity of our resources, the law safeguards the livelihood of Filipino fishers, especially those who daily risk their lives in the contested waters of the West Philippine Sea. These measures turn legal rights into practical protection – protection for the country's fishermen, resources, and maritime future.

Effective enforcement requires more than law; it requires information and technology. These laws encourage greater investment in maritime domain awareness, from satellite monitoring and radar networks to drone surveillance, ensuring that every intrusion or illegal activity in the Philippine's EEZ can be detected, documented, and addressed. Our maritime domain awareness remains limited, fragmented, and reactive. Without these technologies, the legal framework risks being symbolic rather than operational.

Second, the environmental dimension – because the rule of law at sea is not only about sovereignty, but also about stewardship. Both Acts contain provisions that reflect UNCLOS Part XII – the duty of states to protect and preserve the marine environment. Section 11 of RA 12064 and several provisions of RA 12065 prohibit activities that harm marine ecosystems, such as pollution, dumping of waste, or destructive resource extraction. These are not just technical rules, they are legal shields for the country's coral reefs, mangroves, and marine biodiversity. They provide a clearer domestic mandate for agencies such as the Department of Environment and Natural Resources (DENR), PCG, and BFAR to pursue violators, including foreign entities responsible for marine degradation.

This is especially important given the 2016 Arbitral Tribunal's finding that China's massive reclamation and dredging in the Spratly Islands caused severe and irreparable harm to coral reefs – one of the most biodiverse in the world. Through these laws, the Philippines now has both the legal basis and moral authority to prevent such destruction within its maritime zones. Environmental protection, in this sense, becomes not only a matter of ecology but of sovereignty – a defense of the country's natural patrimony against the reckless exploitation of others.

Third, these laws have profound implications for the Philippine's energy future – for the quest to achieve energy independence and national resilience. The Philippine Maritime Zones Act explicitly affirms the country's sovereign rights over the exploration and exploitation of mineral, petroleum, and other non-living resources within the EEZ and continental shelf. This legal clarity provides investor confidence and a stronger foundation for energy exploration projects in the West Philippine Sea and other offshore areas. It defines what is ours to explore – and what lies beyond the reach of foreign interference. At the same time, it sends a clear message: unauthorized exploration or interference by foreign vessels constitutes a violation of Philippine law. This is particularly relevant in areas such as Recto (Reed) Bank – which the 2016 arbitral ruling affirmed as part of the Philippine EEZ.

Through these laws, the Philippine government can better protect legitimate exploration activities and deter unlawful incursions. Of course, these provisions do not eliminate the risk of confrontation. On the contrary, they may heighten tensions with states that continue to assert overlapping or unlawful claims. But this is the essence of legal assertion: it does not provoke instability – it defines order. The Acts replace ambiguity with jurisdiction and confusion with clarity, strengthening the Philippine's hand in future negotiations, partnerships and enforcement actions.

The regional and international dimension of these laws is far-reaching. By enacting RA 12064 and RA 12065, the Philippines has taken a decisive step toward institutionalizing the rule of law in the Indo-Pacific.

This has two aspects – one diplomatic, the other strategic. Diplomatically, these laws enhance the Philippine's credibility and strengthen our alliances with like-minded nations – the United States, Japan, Australia, India, and others – that support a rules-based maritime order. They show that the Philippines are not merely a claimant, but a law-abiding steward of its maritime domain, willing to lead by example in upholding international norms.

Strategically, the laws also serve as deterrents. They provide the legal justification for patrolling our maritime zones, regulating foreign transit, and responding to illegal incursions – not as acts of defiance, but as enforcement of international law.

Of course, with clarity comes confrontation. China continues to reject the 2016 arbitral ruling, and has protested our legislative actions. Yet, by anchoring our position in law rather than politics, the Philippines stands on firmer ground – in diplomacy, in defense, and in moral authority.

Still, we must acknowledge one crucial challenge: enforcement capability. The effectiveness of these laws depends on our ability to patrol and protect our vast maritime zones, an area larger than our land territory. A law, however strong, is only as effective as its implementation. This calls for sustained investment in our Navy, Coast Guard, and surveillance systems, as well as regional cooperation to maintain stability and prevent escalation.

The maritime domain is a field where law meets power – where rules and rights are often tested by realities on the sea. The Philippines today faces immense challenges in enforcing these statutes, arising from China's continued defiance, our own capacity limitations, and the complex regional and geopolitical environment that defines the Indo-Pacific.

The first and most formidable obstacle to implementing our maritime laws lies in China's outright defiance – both of the 2016 arbitral ruling and of the rule of law itself. From the very beginning, China has rejected the PCA award, which invalidated its sweeping "nine-dash line" claims. Following the enactment of RA 12064 and RA 12065 in November 2024, Beijing again summoned our ambassador and protested that these laws "violated its historical rights." This reaction is unsurprising – but it is also revealing. It confirms that what we have enacted challenges the very foundation of China's illegal assertions.

China's defiance is not confined to diplomatic rhetoric. It manifests daily in the West Philippine Sea through a pattern of coercive and aggressive behavior. Chinese Coast Guard and maritime militia vessels continue to make incursions within our EEZ – blocking, shadowing, and harassing Philippine vessels. They encircle contested reefs and shoals with layers of ships – a technique that has become known as "the cabbage strategy" – effectively establishing a de facto exclusion zone; a creeping occupation that undermines our sovereignty without a single shot being fired. We endure physical intimidation in the form of collision incidents, water-cannon attacks, and dangerous maneuvers against our resupply missions to Ayungin Shoal, endangering lives and violating every tenet of international maritime conduct.

Beyond the physical domain, China also employs information warfare – a coordinated effort to discredit the Philippines' legal position and sow division within our public discourse. Through online disinformation, state media narratives, and diplomatic spin, Beijing seeks to create confusion, to "divide and conquer," and to weaken the moral force of our legal position.

This is the environment in which we are asked to implement the rule of law – an environment where legality is met not with compliance, but with coercion and propaganda.

The second major challenge lies within ourselves – in the limitations of our maritime enforcement capacity.

The Philippines are a vast archipelago with one of the world's largest areas of maritime jurisdiction – over 2.2 million square kilometers of EEZ – yet our naval and coast guard assets are painfully insufficient. The Philippine Navy and Coast Guard operate with aging vessels, limited fuel budgets, and logistical gaps that prevent continuous presence in distant waters. This allows foreign incursions and illegal fishing to persist, particularly in the Kalayaan Island Group and Recto Bank. While defense cooperation agreements with allies – including the United States, Japan and Australia – provide training, joint exercises and equipment assistance, the fact remains: sovereignty cannot be subcontracted. We must develop our own indigenous capacity to patrol, to monitor and to enforce. We also face issues of institutional coordination. The new laws give clear mandates, but the enforcement system remains distributed among multiple agencies – the Philippine Navy, the PCG, the BFAR, the Philippine National Police Maritime Group, and the DENR. Without unified command and interoperability, operational response will continue to be slow, fragmented, and often duplicative. This is a challenge of governance, not intent – a reminder that law must be matched by logistics, leadership, and learning.

The third set of challenges is diplomatic and regional in nature. Even within ASEAN, reactions to our new maritime laws have been mixed. While Philippine actions are rooted in UNCLOS and international legality, some neighboring states have expressed reservations. Malaysia, for instance, raised questions regarding how RA 12064 may affect its overlapping maritime claims. These differences complicate efforts to forge a unified ASEAN stance against coercion and could be exploited by China to weaken regional solidarity.

The new laws have inevitably led to heightened tensions with Beijing. Each legislative or enforcement step invites diplomatic protest or maritime retaliation, forcing Manila into a delicate balancing act – asserting rights without provoking escalation.

There is also the foreign policy dimension. The implementation of these laws could expose shifts in our strategic posture – from neutrality to assertion – and such transitions, if not consistently managed, may be exploited by both state and non-state actors. Consistency across administrations is crucial. If future governments waver in implementing these laws, it could send mixed signals that undermine our credibility, both to allies and adversaries. Maritime policy must transcend political cycles; it must be a matter of national continuity, not political convenience.

Finally, we must situate these implementation challenges within the broader geopolitical rivalry of the Indo-Pacific. The strategic competition between the United States and China places the Philippines at the center of regional power dynamics. Beijing views American support for Manila – particularly through joint patrols, defense cooperation, and capacity-building – as a threat to its own influence. This perception may lead to heightened Chinese aggression, increasing the risk of miscalculation or accidental escalation at sea. Nonetheless, our laws send a strategic signal to the world. They affirm that the Philippines stands with the community of nations that believe in a rules-based international order. They show that we are not choosing sides between powers, but choosing the side of law over force, and principle over pressure.

The Philippines has taken its rightful place under the law of the sea. The next challenge is to ensure that law commands respect even in the face of power, and that the rights we have defined in statute are realized in the waters we call our own.

In a region increasingly defined by coercion, gray-zone tactics, and military posturing, the Philippines' enactment of RA 12064 and RA 12065 represents a different kind of strength – the strength of legitimacy, of legal precision, and of principled resolve. These laws demonstrate that in the struggle for maritime stability, the rule of law is not weakness; it is power restrained by principle. They reinforce UNCLOS and the 2016 Arbitral Award as the twin anchors of the maritime order – affirming that peace and security are best preserved when the conduct of states is governed not by force, but by law.

Through these measures, the Philippines has not only fortified its maritime sovereignty; it has also strengthened the very foundation of the rules-based international system – proving that even in a contested geopolitical environment, a small state armed with the law can stand firm against the tides of coercion.

The Philippines' enactment of RA 12064 and RA 12065 provides a strategic and replicable template for other archipelagic and coastal states. It demonstrates that international law gains force when translated into domestic law; legal clarity strengthens enforcement and diplomacy; and the rule of law, when backed by national will and international cooperation, can be a form of strategic power.

The Filipino experience reaffirms that sovereignty in the modern maritime era is not secured by strength alone – it is secured by law, legitimacy, and leadership.

For other nations navigating the same turbulent waters, this lesson endures:

Those who codify their rights in law, uphold them through enforcement, and defend them through diplomacy will shape the maritime order of the future.

Cooperative maritime governance and multilateral partnerships.

Before the passage of the two Acts, maritime cooperation with partners and allies often suffered from ambiguity – a lack of codified legal definitions for maritime zones, transit rules, and enforcement mandates. RA 12064 and RA 12065 have changed that. These statutes now give the Philippines' defense and diplomatic partners – such as the United States, Japan, and Australia – a firm legal basis for engaging in joint patrols, freedom of navigation operations, and maritime domain awareness programs within Philippine waters. When partners operate alongside Philippine agencies, they do so within a framework that is legally coherent and compliant with UNCLOS, reducing political sensitivities and reinforcing legitimacy in joint actions.

Through RA 12065, the Philippines has designated specific Archipelagic Sea Lanes (ASLs) – defined routes through which foreign vessels and aircraft may pass continuously and expeditiously.

These routes are not only navigational corridors but also avenues of cooperation, where coordinated patrols and training exercises can take place under a clearly defined regime of international passage and Philippine sovereignty. The multilateral maritime drills recently held within the country's Exclusive Economic Zone (EEZ) – involving Philippine, American, Japanese, and Australian forces – are direct manifestations of this operational framework.

The codification of prohibited acts and navigational obligations ensures uniformity of rules across all partners. This standardization fosters interoperability, enabling seamless coordination during joint maritime operations, search and rescue missions, and disaster response efforts within Philippine waters. In essence, legal precision has now become the enabler of international cooperation – turning the Philippines' assertion of rights into a platform for shared maritime governance.

The Philippines' maritime partnerships must not be confined to security. They also extend to the sustainable use and protection of the seas – an area where RA 12064 and RA 12065 provide fertile ground for collaboration.

By explicitly defining the Philippines' sovereign rights over living resources within its EEZ, RA 12064 provides the legal foundation for bilateral and multilateral fisheries agreements. These agreements can address the pervasive challenge of illegal, unreported, and unregulated (IUU) fishing, which undermines both economic livelihoods and marine ecosystems. Shared patrols, coordinated licensing, and intelligence exchange mechanisms with neighboring states – such as Indonesia, Malaysia, and Vietnam – can all flow from this legal framework.

Both laws also affirm the Philippines' commitment to marine environmental protection, prohibiting pollution, unauthorized research and destructive activities. These provisions create opportunities for joint scientific expeditions, marine biodiversity monitoring, and climate resilience projects, supported by partners like the European Union and ASEAN Centre for Biodiversity.

In an era of ecological vulnerability, such partnerships embody UNCLOS Part XII on the protection and preservation of the marine environment. The transition from competition to cooperation, particularly in marine conservation and fisheries governance, demonstrates that shared stewardship can coexist with sovereign assertion.

At the diplomatic level, RA 12064 and RA 12065 strengthen the Philippines' capacity to lead – not merely to participate – in regional maritime governance. By adhering to UNCLOS and the arbitral ruling, the Philippines positions itself as a credible advocate of the rules-based international order. This credibility fortifies alliances with like-minded states that value freedom of navigation and respect for sovereign equality. The Philippines' legislative actions serve as a counter-narrative to unilateralism, reaffirming that international law remains the cornerstone of peace and cooperation in the Indo-Pacific.

The legal clarity provided by these statutes enhances the Philippines' influence in ASEAN mechanisms, including the ASEAN Regional Forum, the East Asia Summit, and the ASEAN Defense Ministers' Meeting-Plus Maritime Security Working Group. Within these forums, the Philippines can now articulate positions rooted in law, advocate for cooperative enforcement mechanisms, and strengthen calls for a binding Code of Conduct in the South China Sea.

The laws institutionalize the Philippines' commitment to peaceful dispute settlement under Part XV of UNCLOS, reinforcing the legitimacy of international arbitration and judicial remedies as tools of statecraft. In diplomacy as in law, clarity commands respect. These laws give the Philippines both moral and legal authority in regional deliberations.

A Badge of Honor

When the Philippines enacted the Maritime Zones Act and the Archipelagic Sea Lanes Act, we knew that these measures would not only clarify our maritime rights but also test our national resolve. The reaction from China was swift, sharp, and telling. It came in the form of diplomatic condemnation – and, more significantly, personal sanctions imposed against those of us who authored and defended these laws.

In July 2025, China's Foreign Ministry issued a statement condemning me and banning me from ever travelling to mainland China, Hong Kong or Macao. "For quite some time," the Foreign Ministry statement said, "driven by selfish interests, a handful of anti-China politicians in the Philippines have made malicious remarks and moves on issues related to China that are detrimental to China's interests and China-Philippines relations. The Chinese government is firmly resolved to defend national sovereignty, security, and development interests. China decides to impose sanctions on former Philippines senator Francis Tolentino for his egregious conduct on China-related issues and prohibit him from entering the Chinese mainland, Hong Kong and Macao."[103]

In response, I issued a statement of my own.

“I acknowledge the sanctions imposed on me by China for defending the rights, dignity, and sovereignty of the Filipino people in the West Philippine Sea. I have fought – and will continue to fight – for what rightfully belongs to our nation. This sanction is a badge of honor and a testament to my unwavering commitment to protect our national interest and our people’s dignity.

“I stand firmly with the Philippine Navy, the Philippine Coast Guard, and our brave fishermen who depend on these waters for their livelihood.

“No foreign power can silence me or weaken my resolve to uphold our sovereignty. I am, and will always be, proud to be a Filipino.”

My fellow senators came to my defense. "Since when has crafting legislation that asserts our sovereign rights been considered egregious conduct?" asked Senate President Pro Tempore Jinggoy Estrada. "It is appalling that efforts to defend our territorial claims are now being branded as 'egregious conduct.' China should be ashamed." 104

These sanctions are, to me, truly a “badge of honor.”

But what do these sanctions really mean?

They reveal a paradox – a paradox where coercion becomes confession, and punishment becomes proof. For in trying to suppress our voice, these sanctions have only amplified our message.

These actions were framed as punitive, but in truth, they were a tacit recognition of influence.

For nearly a decade, Beijing dismissed the 2016 Arbitral Award as, and I quote, *"a piece of waste paper."* Yet, when the Philippines translated that award into binding domestic law, the response changed. China moved from words to sanctions, from denial to reaction. That alone reveals the power of codification – the strength that lies in transforming an international judgment into a concrete, enforceable statute. By sanctioning a legislator instead of challenging the law itself, China acknowledged something profound: that legal legitimacy carries a force that coercion cannot overcome. It cannot defeat a statute grounded in UNCLOS, endorsed by the international community, and upheld by the rule of law. The contrast is clear – while China wields coercive power, the Philippines wields legal authority.

The sanctions imposed were, in effect, a price placed upon principle. They reflect how seriously China views the act of codifying the arbitral award into domestic legislation. For them, it was not a symbolic act – it was an act of sovereign defiance by the Philippines; an assertion of national dignity through law. And if there is a price for that, then it is one the Filipino nation is willing to pay.

This brings us to the paradox of Beijing's reaction. The more it tries to silence, the louder the echo becomes. The more it seeks to intimidate, the more it validates our cause.

Within its borders, China maintains a controlled narrative – one that denies the legitimacy of both the arbitral award and our new laws. Its state media censors discussion of UNCLOS compliance, portraying our legislation as "provocative" or "illegal." To its own citizens, it projects an illusion of total control. But truth cannot be contained by censorship – it travels farther than any border.

On the world stage, the sanctions backfired. Rather than isolating the Philippines, they amplified our message – that our actions are rooted in international law, not in confrontation. They drew attention from governments, think tanks, and legal experts across continents who now cite the Philippine experience as a model for domestic implementation of UNCLOS. The global community took notice that the sanctions were directed not at military aggression, but at legislative action – the peaceful exercise of sovereignty through law. This prompted renewed support for the Philippines from allies and partners who, too, uphold a rules-based maritime order.

These acts of retaliation have unmasked Beijing's true strategy – the use of coercion when the law does not favor it. In doing so, China has inadvertently strengthened the moral and diplomatic position of the Philippines. It has turned the spotlight on its own disregard for UNCLOS and further isolated itself within the international legal community.

Let me say candidly: for any public servant, to be sanctioned for defending the rule of law is not a punishment – it is a badge of honor. It is proof that what we have done matters, that our laws have weight, and that our words have consequence.

In this paradox lies an unexpected strength. The sanctions, intended as deterrence, have become a signal – to our allies, to our region, and to the world. They signal that the Philippines are not merely asserting claims, but institutionalizing them through legitimate lawmaking. They demonstrate that a small nation, armed with the power of law and principle, can confront the excesses of a greater power without abandoning diplomacy or peace. They affirm that when law replaces force, and when reason replaces intimidation, the moral victory belongs to those who stand by UNCLOS.

The truth is, these sanctions have made the laws more visible, the ruling more relevant, and our message more resonant. In seeking to diminish our resolve, China has only magnified our determination. In trying to silence a voice, it has given that voice a global audience.

History has shown us that power built on intimidation is fleeting, but power grounded in law endures. The sanctions of 2025 will be remembered not as a story of suppression, but as an affirmation of legitimacy – a moment when our laws, born from UNCLOS and the 2016 Arbitral Award, proved too powerful to ignore. These laws are not merely Philippine statutes. They are symbols of a global truth – that the sea, like justice, must remain free, fair, and governed by law. And if upholding that truth provokes sanctions, then let those sanctions stand as proof that we are doing what is right.

Because, in the end, the real power does not belong to those who impose sanctions, but to those who write the laws that endure beyond them.

The Philippines' success in translating international law into domestic law has not gone unnoticed. Other states – coastal and archipelagic alike – are closely watching.

Vietnam has long taken a careful and quiet approach to maritime disputes, balancing nationalism with pragmatism. Yet our example – the peaceful codification of sovereign rights under UNCLOS – could encourage Hanoi to take a more assertive legal stance, grounding its claims more explicitly in international law. The precedent we set offers a roadmap for legal, rather than military, assertion.

Indonesia, as the world's largest archipelagic state, shares many of our challenges – from foreign incursions to fishing disputes. Jakarta has designated some archipelagic sea lanes, but not all. The Philippine model may well encourage Indonesia to complete its archipelagic sea lanes system and fortify its maritime enforcement framework, ensuring that its vast seas remain under effective control.

Malaysia's reaction has been mixed – protesting our reference to Sabah, yet acknowledging the legal soundness of our framework. The Philippines' proactive approach may motivate Malaysia to clarify its own maritime boundaries and strengthen domestic enforcement, further contributing to a regional convergence toward legal certainty.

What we are witnessing is the potential beginning of a "legislative wave" in Southeast Asia – a wave of codification and clarity inspired by the Philippine example. These new laws also pave the way for multilateral maritime cooperation. They could provide the foundation for a stronger ASEAN maritime governance regime – one grounded in UNCLOS, transparency, and cooperation, rather than ambiguity and rivalry.

By clarifying where our entitlements begin and end, we help create the legal stability necessary for dialogue, negotiation, and eventually, shared stewardship of the seas. Through clear law, we make cooperation possible.

Law without enforcement is a map without motion. To defend our maritime future, we must match our legal clarity with operational readiness. These laws also reshape our role in the Indo-Pacific. They reaffirm that the Philippines stands firmly on the side of international law, even as great power competition intensifies.

We expect continued political and economic pressure from those who reject the arbitral ruling. But the Philippines will meet this challenge not with provocation, but with principle – not through force, but through fidelity to law.

The legal clarity provided by these laws strengthens our partnerships with the United States, Japan, Australia, and other like-minded nations. Cooperative patrols, capacity-building, and defense agreements are now grounded not just in politics, but in law.

Within the regional context, our adherence to international law reinforces ASEAN centrality – the belief that Southeast Asian nations must lead through dialogue, consensus, and lawful conduct, not through coercion or fragmentation.

The enactment of these laws transforms the Philippines from a participant in the maritime legal order to a leader in shaping it. The Philippines' message to the world is simple. Sovereignty can be asserted peacefully. Rights can be defended lawfully. Power can be exercised responsibly. These principles – embodied in the Philippine Maritime Zones Act and Archipelagic Sea Lanes Act – show that even in a contested environment, an archipelagic state can protect its interests through law, not through force. And this, perhaps, is the greatest lesson we offer to our region and to the world: that courage in the 21st century is measured not by the size of one's fleet, but by the strength of one's laws and by the steadfastness with which a nation upholds them.

I hope that the Filipino people, especially Filipino youth, will come to understand that the passing of these vital Acts was undertaken for their future – the future of all Filipinos. The fight for the West Philippine Sea is not the fight of a few people, but the fight of all freedom-loving individuals. The Acts have the power to usher in a future in which the birthright of all Filipinos – the waters that surround and protect them and provide them with food and vital resources – is secured and protected from foreign powers who covet these precious waters for themselves. This may not come about in my lifetime, but the enduring power of the law is such that I truly believe the outcome for future generations is now secured.

As we look to this future, let us remember: The rule of law is not a shield we carry only in times of peace. It is the compass that guides us through conflict, uncertainty, and change. The Philippines has chosen its course – a course grounded in international law, national dignity, and regional responsibility. Others may soon follow, inspired by what we have done, measured by what we continue to defend.

The passage of these laws is not just a Philippine story. It is a story of how a nation, bound by history and surrounded by sea, turned its geography into strength and its laws into leadership. In a world where the rule of force seeks to drown the rule of law, the Philippines stands as proof that justice, like the tide, will always rise.

I would like to conclude this book with a poem: Epistle to the Filipino People

Epistle to the Filipino People

Mga Minamahal Kong Kababayan

I do not write to you
from a podium.

I write from a shoreline
that faces west.

You have read the headlines.
You have seen the footage –
boats, barriers,
water rising against hulls.

But I want you to remember
what came before the noise.

The maps in quiet ink.
The fishermen at dawn.
The reef rising patient
above tide.

This shoal is not

an abstract dispute.

It is a place your fathers sailed to

without asking permission.

It is a horizon measured

In diesel and faith.

Some will say

it is too small to matter.

1.8 meters above water.

Barely visible on a clear day.

But we are an island people.

We know that what rises only slightly

can still anchor a nation.

I have stood in Masinloc
and listened to widows speak softly.

I have watched young men
push Bangkas back into sea
because retreat is not inheritance.

This is not a call to anger.
Anger is brief.
This is a call to memory.
Memory lasts longer than spray.

We must remain steady.
Steadier than steel.

We must remain lawful.
Stronger than provocation.

We must remain patient.
Longer than pressure.

For sovereignty is not

how loudly we answer, but how consistently

we return.

Mahal kong Kababayan, the sea that surrounds us

is not merely border.

It is breath.

Guard it without hatred.

Defend it without fury.

Hold it without fear.

And when you look west

across the West Philippine Sea at dusk,

remember Scarborough Shoal –

not large upon the earth,

yet enduring upon the soul of a Nation.

With you always

Francis "Tol" Tolentino

Notes

Introduction

[1] Richard Spratly, "Nautical Notices: Land Reef and Spratly Island — China Sea," T*he Nautical Magazine and Naval Chronicle* 12 (1843): 697, https://archive.org/details/the-nautical-magazine-1843/page/695/mode/1up.
[2] “China Vessel ‘Deliberately Rammed’ PH Ship Providing Cover for Fishermen: PCG”, *ABS-CBN News*, October 12, 2025, https://www.abs-cbn.com/news/nation/2025/10/12/china-vessel-deliberately-rammed-philippine-ship-pcg-1125.
[3] “Allies, Partners Condemn Chinese Coercion of Philippine Vessels”, *Indo-Pacific Defense Forum*, October 26, 2025, https://ipdefenseforum.com/2025/10/allies-partners-condemn-chinas-coercion-of-philippine-vessels/.
[4] *ABS-CBN News*, “China Vessel ‘Deliberately Rammed’.”
[5] "China and the Philippines Both Plant Their Flags on the Same Disputed Sandbar," *NBC News*, April 29, 2025, https://www.nbcnews.com/world/china/china-philippines-both-plant-flags-disputed-sandbar-rcna203256.
[6] U.S. Department of State, "U.S. Statement on Dangerous Chinese Actions in the South China Sea," October 13, 2025, https://www.state.gov/releases/office-of-the-spokesperson/2025/10/u-s-statement-on-dangerous-chinese-actions-in-the-south-china-sea.
[7] Dexter Cabalza et al., “PH to Protest China’s Attack on BFAR Vessel,” *Philippine Daily Inquirer,* October 13, 2025, https://www.inquirer.net/457638/ph-to-protest-chinas-attack-on-bfar-vessel/.

1: Mischief on Mischief Reef

[8] United Nations Convention on the Law of the Sea, art. 55–57, opened for signature December 10, 1982, 1833 U.N.T.S. 397 (entered into force November 16, 1994).

[9] Bill Hayton, *The South China Sea: The Struggle for Power in Asia* (New Haven and London: Yale University Press, 2014), 85-86.

[10] B. Raman, "The Battle for Mischief Reef: Chinese Territorial Assertions: The Case of the Mischief Reef," Institute for Topical Studies, Chennai. January 14, 1999. Originally published at http://www.warfighter.org/mischief.html. Archived at ALC Press, https://alcpress.org/mirrors/spratly/index.html.

[11] Ramon Farolan, "Mischievous China Makes More Mischief," *Inquirer Opinion*, January 18, 2016, https://opinion.inquirer.net/92127/mischievous-china-makes-more-mischief.

[12] B. Raman, "The Battle for Mischief Reef".

[13] Raman, "The Battle for Mischief Reef."

[14] Raman, "The Battle for Mischief Reef".

[15] Toshi Yoshihara, "The 1974 Paracels Sea Battle: A Campaign Appraisal," *Naval War College Review* 69, no. 2 (Spring 2016): 41–65, https://digital-commons.usnwc.edu/nwc-review/vol69/iss2/6.

[16] Daniel Hartnett, "The Father of the Modern Chinese Navy – Liu Huaqing," Center for International Maritime Security, October 8, 2014, https://cimsec.org/father-modern-chinese-navy-liu-huaqing/.

[17] Marco Hernandez, Dan Bland, and Michael Kassay, "Conflicting Claims," *South China Morning Post*, 2016,

https://multimedia.scmp.com/2016/southChinaSea/explore.html.

[18] M. Taylor Fravel, "China's Strategy in the South China Sea," *Contemporary Southeast Asia* 33, no. 3 (2011): 298.

[19] Lt. Cmdr. Jeff W. Benson, USN, "South China Sea: A History of Armed Conflict," USNI News, June 20, 2012, https://news.usni.org/2012/06/20/south-china-sea-history-armed-conflict.

[20] Hayton, *The South China Sea*, 83.

[21] Legends Lore, "The 1988 Naval Battle: China's Victory at Chigua Reef," YouTube video, 2:50", accessed November 18, 2025, https://www.youtube.com/watch?v=lpNRjavVjm4.

[22] Fravel, "China's Strategy," 298.

[23] Benson, "South China Sea."

[24] ASEAN, "ASEAN Declaration on the South China Sea," Manila, Philippines, July 22, 1992, https://asean.org/asean-declaration-on-the-south-china-sea-manila-philippines-22-july-1992/.

2: Lines in the Sea

[25] Associated Press, "China Has Reclaimed 3,200 Acres in the South China Sea, Says Pentagon," *Guardian*, May 13, 2016, https://www.theguardian.com/world/2016/may/13/pentagon-report-china-reclaimed-3200-acres-south-china-sea.

[26] "China Preps Spratlys for Military Aircraft," Asia Maritime Transparency Initiative, Center for Strategic and International Studies, October 3, 2016, https://amti.csis.org/build-it-and-they-will-come/.

[27] "China's Big Three Near Completion," Asia Maritime Transparency Initiative, Center for Strategic and International Studies, originally published March 27, 2017, updated June 29, 2017, https://amti.csis.org/chinas-big-three-near-completion/.

[28] Harry B. Harris Jr., "Speech Delivered to the Australian Strategic Policy Institute" (speech, Canberra, Australia, March 31, 2015), Commander, US Pacific Fleet, http://www.cpf.navy.mil/leaders/harry-harris/speeches/2015/03/ASPI-Australia.pdf, archived at https://web.archive.org/web/20160529035123/http://www.cpf.navy.mil/leaders/harry-harris/speeches/2015/03/ASPI-Australia.pdf.

[29] U.S. Department of State, Bureau of Oceans and International Environmental and Scientific Affairs, *Limits in the Seas, No. 143: China: Maritime Claims in the South China Sea* (Washington, DC: U.S. Department of State, 2014), https://www.state.gov/wp-content/uploads/2019/10/LIS-143.pdf.

[30] Bill Hayton in conversation with the author.

[31] Bill Hayton, "The Modern Origins of China's South China Sea Claims: Maps, Misunderstandings and the Maritime Geobody," *Modern China* 45, no. 2 (2019): 136.

[32] Li Zhun, quoted in Hayton, "The Modern Origins,"132.

[33] Hayton, "The Modern Origins," 133.

[34] Ibid., 137–138.

[35] Ibid., 147.

[36] Ibid., 142.

[37] Chris P. C. Chung, "Drawing the U-Shaped Line: China's Claim to the South China Sea, 1946-1974," *Modern China* 42, no. 1 (2016): 42.

[38] Hayton, "The Modern Origins," 127.

3: Recto Bank – The Battle for Oil and Gas

[39] Hayton, *South China Sea*, 45.
[40] Paterno R. Esmaquel, II "Recto Bank: Why China covets what belongs to the Philippines," *Rappler*, June 14, 2023. https://www.rappler.com/newsbreak/iq/233069-reasons-china-covets-recto-bank-philippines/
[41] Ian Storey, "China and the Philippines: Implications of the Reed Bank Incident," *The Jamestown Foundation*, June 5, 2011, https://jamestown.org/program/china-and-the-philippines-implications-of-the-reed-bank-incident/
[42] Bill Hayton, *The South China Sea*, 145.
[43] "Recto Bank: Why China Covets," *Rappler*, June 14, 2023.
[44] VERA Files, "VERA FILES FACT CHECK: Apology from Chinese association falsely claims Recto Bank is China territory," April 5, 2023, https://verafiles.org/articles/vera-files-fact-check-apology-chinese-association-falsely-cl.
[45] "Recto Bank: Why China Covets," *Rappler*, June 14, 2023.
[46] "US Agency Sees Huge Oil, Gas Potential in Spratlys," *The Philippine Star*, February 11, 2013, https://www.philstar.com/business/2013/02/11/907251/us-agency-sees-huge-oil-gas-potential-spratlys.
[47] "Seismic Indicates Giant Gas at Sampaguita," *Oil & Gas Journal*, September 26, 2006.
[48] Antonio Carpio, *The South China Sea/West Philippine Sea Dispute,* ebook ver. 1.0 (self-pub., May 4, 2017), https://murillovelardemap.com/wp-content/uploads/2017/05/SCS-WPSDisputeNon-Interactive.pdf.

[49] "Recto Bank: Why China Covets," Rappler.

[50] John Mark Bautista, "Oil and gas exploration in the Philippines," *GeoExpro*, June 20, 2024, https://geoexpro.com/oil-and-gas-exploration-in-the-philippines/.

[51] Hayton, *The South China Sea*, 145–146.

[52] Rambo Talabong and Sofia Tomacruz, "The Sinking of Gem-Ver: Barko! May babanggang barko!" *Rappler*, July 10, 2019, https://www.rappler.com/newsbreak/in-depth/234304-there-is-a-ship-about-hit-sinking-gem-ver-recto-bank-series-part-1/.

[53] Ellen Tordesillas, "Why is there a Chinese military vessel in Reed Bank?" *VERA Files*, June 17, 2019, https://verafiles.org/articles/why-there-chinese-military-vessel-reed-bank.

[54] Stephen Stashwick, "Chinese Vessel Rams, Sinks Philippine Fishing Boat in Reed Bank," *The Diplomat*, June 14, 2019, https://thediplomat.com/2019/06/chinese-vessel-rams-sinks-philippine-fishing-boat-in-reed-bank/.

[55] Renato Cruz de Castro, "Incident at Reed Bank: A Crisis in the Philippines' China Policy," *Asia Maritime Transparency Initiative*, June 20, 2019, https://amti.csis.org/incident-at-reed-bank-a-crisis-in-the-philippines-china-policy/.

[56] Pia Lee-Brago, "Chinese Fishing Vessel Owner Apologizes for Recto Bank Incident," *The Philippine Star*, August 29, 2019, https://www.philstar.com/headlines/2019/08/29/1947380/chinese-fishing-vessel-owner-apologizes-recto-bank-incident.

[57] Ellen Tordesillas, "Roque is best advisor to Duterte on joint exploration with China," *VERA Files*, March 9, 2018, https://verafiles.org/articles/roque-best-adviser-duterte-joint-exploration-china

[58] Ellen Tordesillas, "Recalling JMSU," *VERA Files*, April 27, 2017, https://verafiles.org/articles/recalling-jmsu

[59] Ministry of Foreign Affairs of the People's Republic of China, "Memorandum of Understanding on Cooperation on Oil and Gas Development between the Government of the People's Republic of China and the Government of the Republic of the Philippines," November 20, 2018, https://www.fmprc.gov.cn/nanhai/eng/zcfg_1/201811/t20181127_8523697.htm.

[60] Camille Elemia, "China 'committed' to Joint Oil Exploration with Philippines Despite Court Ruling," December 1, 2023, *Radio Free Asia*, https://amti.csis.org/a-philippine-china-deal-on-joint-development-in-the-making/.

[61] Supreme Court of the Philippines, "SC Declares Unconstitutional the Joint Marine Seismic Undertaking Among Philippine, Vietnamese, and Chinese Oil Firms," January 10, 2023, https://sc.judiciary.gov.ph/sc-declares-unconstitutional-the-joint-marine-seismic-undertaking-among-philippine-vietnamese-and-chinese-oil-firms/.

4: The Standoff at Panatag

[62] Jay L. Batongbacal, "Bajo de Masinloc (Scarborough Shoal): Less-Known Facts vs. Published Fiction" (lecture, Cartographic Exhibit Forum, De La Salle University, Manila, September 26, 2014), accessed January 17, 2026, https://imoa.ph/bajo-de-masinloc-scarborough-shoal-less-known-facts-vs-published-fiction/.

[63] Kathleen de Villa, "What Went Before: Panatag Shoal Standoff," *Inquirer.net*, February 17, 2022, https://newsinfo.inquirer.net/1421704/what-went-before-panatag-shoal-standoff.

[64] Marites Vitug, *Rock Solid: How the Philippines Won Its Maritime Case against China* (Quezon City: Ateneo de Manila University Press, 2018), 79–82, Kindle.

[65] Michael Green et al., "Scarborough Shoal Standoff," *Asia Maritime Transparency Initiative* Counter-Coercion Series, May 22, 2017, https://amti.csis.org/counter-co-scarborough-standoff/

[66] Kathleen de Villa, "What Went Before."

[67] Michael Green et al., "Scarborough Shoal."

[68] Vitug, *Rock Solid*, 116–117, Kindle.

[69] Michael Green et al., "Scarborough Shoal."

[70] Ibid., 120.

[71] Ely Ratner, "Learning the Lessons of Scarborough Reef," *The National Interest*, November 21, 2013, https://nationalinterest.org/feature/learning-the-lessons-scarborough-reef-9442.

[72] "PH Bananas Rotting in Chinese Ports," *Philippine Daily Inquirer*, May 12, 2012, https://newsinfo.inquirer.net/191951/ph-bananas-rotting-in-chinese-ports.

[73] Amando Doronila, "Dispute Becomes Economic," *Philippine Daily Inquirer*, May 14, 2012, https://opinion.inquirer.net/28681/dispute-becomes-economic.

[74] Floyd Whaley, "US Reaffirms Defense of Philippines in Standoff with China," *New York Times*, May 1, 2012, https://www.nytimes.com/2012/05/02/world/asia/us-reaffirms-defense-of-philippines-in-standoff-with-china.html#:~:text=del%20Rosario%20responded:%20%E2%80%9CThey%20have,political%20context%2C%E2%80%9D%20he%20said.

[75] Geoff Dyer and Demetri Sevastopulo , "US Strategists Face Dilemma Over Beijing Claim in South China Sea," *Financial Times*, July 10, 2014.
[76] Ellen Tordesillas, "The back channels: Trillanes, US and Pangilinan," *VERA Files*, September 21, 2012, https://verafiles.org/articles/the-back-channels-trillanes-us-and-pangilinan#:~:text=Days%20before%20President%20Aquino%20left,this%20agreement%20in%20several%20statements.
[77] Michael Green et al., "Scarborough Shoal."
[78] Ellen Tordesillas, "The Back Channels."
[79] Gil C. Cabacungan, "Aquino's back channel to China is Trillanes," *Philippine Daily Inquirer*, September 19, 2012, https://globalnation.inquirer.net/50558/aquinos-back-channel-to-china-is-trillanes.
[80] Ratner, "Learning the Lessons."
[81] Antonio T. Carpio, "Law and Justice in the West Philippine Sea," *Rappler*, December 12, 2020, https://www.rappler.com/voices/thought-leaders/opinion-law-justice-west-philippine-sea/

5: The Constitution of the Oceans

[82] Arvid Pardo, "Examination of the Question of the Reservation Exclusively for Peaceful Purposes of the Sea-Bed and the Ocean Floor, and the Subsoil Thereof, Underlying the High Seas Beyond the Limits of Present National Jurisdiction, and the Use of Their Resources in the Interests of Mankind," Statement to the First Committee of the UN General Assembly, 22nd Session, 1515th meeting, UN Doc. A/C.1/PV.1515 (November 1, 1967),

https://www.un.org/depts/los/convention_agreements/texts/pardo_ga1967.pdf.

[83] United Nations, Convention on the Continental Shelf, April 29, 1958, United Nations Treaty Series, vol. 499, p. 311, https://legal.un.org/ilc/texts/instruments/english/conventions/8_1_1958_continental_shelf.pdf.

[84] Philippine Department of Foreign Affairs, "The Archipelagic Doctrine," MANA Mo (Maritime and Ocean Affairs - National Awareness Months of Observance), accessed January 28, 2026, https://sites.google.com/dfa.gov.ph/manamo/the-archipelagic-doctrine.

[85] Vitug, *Rock Solid*, 162.

[86] Zheng Wang, "China and UNCLOS: An Inconvenient History," *The Diplomat*, July 11, 2016, https://thediplomat.com/2016/07/china-and-unclos-an-inconvenient-history/.

[87] James Kraska, "The Nine Ironies of the South China Sea Mess," *The Diplomat*, September 17, 2015, https://thediplomat.com/2015/09/the-nine-ironies-of-the-south-china-sea-mess/.

[88] James Kraska, "The Nine Ironies."

[89] Philippines, *Constitution of the Republic of the Philippines (*1987), Official Gazette, https://www.officialgazette.gov.ph/constitutions/the-1987-constitution-of-the-republic-of-the-philippines/.

[90] Carpio, "Law and Justice in the West Philippine Sea."

[91] World Economic Forum,"Here's Why the UN Convention on the Law of the Sea (UNCLOS) Needs an Overhaul," December 14, 2022, https://www.weforum.org/stories/2022/12/here-s-why-un-law-sea-overhaul/.

6: The Road to the Hague

[92] Vitug, *Rock Solid*,206.

[93] Albert F. del Rosario, "Statement by Secretary of Foreign Affairs Albert del Rosario on the UNCLOS Arbitral Proceedings against China to Achieve a Peaceful and Durable Solution to the Dispute in the WPS," Philippine Embassy Tokyo, January 22, 2013, https://tokyo.philembassy.net/statement-by-secretary-of-foreign-affairs-albert-del-rosario-on-the-unclos-arbitral-proceedings-against-china-to-achieve-a-peaceful-and-durable-solution-to-the-dispute-in-the-wps/

[94] "China Rejects Philippines' Arbitral Request," *China Daily*, February 19, 2013, http://www.chinadaily.com.cn/china/2013-02/19/content_16238133.htm.

[95] People's Republic of China, Ministry of Foreign Affairs, "Position Paper of the Government of the People's Republic of China on the Matter of Jurisdiction in the South China Sea Arbitration Initiated by the Republic of the Philippines," December 7, 2014, https://www.fmprc.gov.cn/eng/gjhdq_665435/2675_665437/2762_663528/2763_663530/202406/t20240607_11412222.html.

7: The Arbitral Ruling

[96] Tom Phillips et al., "Beijing Rejects Tribunal's Ruling in South China Sea Case," *The Guardian*, July 12, 2016, https://www.theguardian.com/world/2016/jul/12/philippines-wins-south-china-sea-case-against-china

[97] "'Just a Piece of Paper': Duterte Says He Will 'Throw Away' Philippines' Arbitral Win vs China," *The Philippine Star*, May 6, 2021, https://www.philstar.com/headlines/2021/05/06/2096287/.

8: From Tagaytay to the Senate

[98] Sofia Tomacruz, "China's Vessels Swarming Julian Felipe Reef, West PH Sea," *Rappler*, April 30, 2021, https://www.rappler.com/newsbreak/iq/timeline-china-vessels-julian-felipe-reef-west-philippine-sea-2021/

[99] Frances Mangosing, "Chinese ship 'spied on PH-US war games'," *Philippine Daily Inquirer*, March 15, 2022, https://newsinfo.inquirer.net/1568878/sino-ship-spied-on-ph-us-war-games

11: The Struggle Continues

[100] Kurt Dela Peña, "China's Nine-Dash Line: A Dangerous Fiction Even in the Movies," *The Philippine Daily Inquirer*, July 7, 2023, https://newsinfo.inquirer.net/1798710/chinas-nine-dash-line-a-dangerous-fiction-even-in-the-movies

[101] Bill Hayton in conversation with the author.

12: Enough is Enough

[102] Pia Lee-Brago, "Spy Handlers Asked for Info on Troops in West Philippine Sea," *The Philippine Star*, March 9, 2026, https://www.philstar.com/headlines/2026/03/09/2513023/spy-handlers-asked-info-troops-west-philippine-sea

13: The Enduring Power of Law

[103] Ministry of Foreign Affairs of the People's Republic of China, "Foreign Ministry Spokesperson Announces Sanctions on the Philippines' Former Senator Francis Tolentino," July 1, 2025, https://www.fmprc.gov.cn/eng/xw/fyrbt/fyrbt/202507/t20250701_11662115.html.

[104] Pia Lee-Brago, "China Bars Tolentino for 'Egregious Conduct'," *The Philippine Star*, July 2, 2025, https://www.philstar.com/headlines/2025/07/02/2454811/china-bars-tolentino-egregious-conduct.

www.ingramcontent.com/pod-product-compliance
Lightning Source LLC
LaVergne TN
LVHW090603110826
845146LV00001B/244

* 9 7 9 8 9 9 3 8 6 4 6 7 9 *